David George Ritchie

Darwinism and Politics

David George Ritchie

Darwinism and Politics

ISBN/EAN: 9783337077914

Printed in Europe, USA, Canada, Australia, Japan

Cover: Foto ©Suzi / pixelio.de

More available books at **www.hansebooks.com**

DARWINISM AND POLITICS.

BY

DAVID G. RITCHIE, M.A.,

Fellow and Tutor of Jesus College, Oxford.

SECOND EDITION, WITH TWO ADDITIONAL ESSAYS

ON

HUMAN EVOLUTION.

LONDON:

SWAN SONNENSCHEIN & CO.,

PATERNOSTER SQUARE.

1891

IT may perhaps obviate some objections if I state here in one sentence what my main thesis is, although indeed I should have thought that it admitted of no misunderstanding. In the essay entitled *Darwinism and Politics*, now reprinted with a few verbal alterations, I seek to prove that *The theory of Natural Selection (in the form in which alone it can properly be applied to human society) lends no support to the political dogma of Laissez faire.* The second and third essays, which are now added to the original essay, deal with the parenthetic clause, and attempt to answer the question : *In what form, if in any, can the theory of Natural Selection properly be applied to the intellectual, moral and social development of man ?* The second essay is a criticism of the last chapter of Mr. A. R. Wallace's *Darwinism*, and has already appeared in the *Westminster Review*. The third has been suggested by some " Anti-evolutionist " objections of Dr. Emil Reich. It is, I think, always convenient, and especially in a brief treatment of a subject, to have definite objections to deal with and to use a dialectic method instead of the formal exposition more appropriate to an elaborate and systematic treatise.

A critic in the *Academy* complains that he cannot grasp the exact object of my little book. Well, I do not think I really can do anything more to help him or any one else who feels a similar difficulty. He also complains of my using the term "Darwinism" for the doctrine of Evolution. I have used the term "Darwinism" not, as he suggests, in imitation of the German habit, but simply because I mean it. I am dealing with the scientific theory of Natural Selection, and not with all those metaphysical hypotheses which go under the name of Evolution. On this matter a little has been said at the beginning of the second essay.

My friend, Mr. E. B. Poulton (to whom, more than to any man or book I am indebted for my biological premises, though of course I must not hold him responsible for all the sociological and practical conclusions I have ventured to draw), has just called my attention to a little work by Mr. W. Platt Ball, entitled, *Are the Effects of Use and Disuse inherited?* (London, 1890). Mr. Ball argues with great force against Mr. Herbert Spencer and against the Lamarckianism surviving in Darwin, that the theory of "Use-inheritance" (*i.e.* the direct inheritance of the effects of use and disuse in kind) is "unnecessary, unproven and improbable:" and he draws the important practical inference that for the improvement of human society reliance on use-inheritance is misplaced. With all this I entirely agree. But when Mr. Ball goes on to treat his arguments against private philanthropy as if they were also valid against systematic action on the part of the State, I must dissent in the strongest manner. Let me quote a few sentences from the "Preface" and the "Conclusion" of Mr. Ball's work :—

"Civilisation largely sets aside the harsh but ultimately salutary action of the great law of Natural Selection without providing an efficient substitute for preventing degeneracy. The substitute on which moralists and legislators rely—if they think on the matter at all—is the cumulative inheritance of the beneficial effects of education, training, habits, institutions and so forth—the inheritance, in short, of acquired characters, or of the effects of use and disuse" (p. vii).

"The selective influences by which our present high level has been reached and maintained may well be modified [How much does Mr. Ball mean by that?], but they must not be abandoned or reversed in the rash expectation that State education, or State feeding of children, or State housing of the poor, or any amount of State socialism or public or private philanthropy will prove permanently satisfactory substitutes. If ruinous deterioration and other more immediate evils are to be avoided, the race must still be to the swift and the battle to the strong. The healthy Individualism so earnestly championed by Mr. Spencer must be allowed free play" (p. 155).

What I have said on pp. 53, 54 anticipates the way in which I should meet this argument. Just because it is "not proven" that acquired characteristics are transmitted, we cannot trust for the improvement of the race to the moralisation of stray individuals now (however desirable and necessary that is in itself): we must reform institutions so that the new individuals shall be born into healthy surroundings. The training process has always to be performed afresh. In the course of his arguments against the Lamarckian doctrine, Mr. Ball has shown how much can be done by education and imitation, apart from heredity, even among the social insects, how very much more among human beings. Of this fact we must make all the use we can. Of course it will make a great difference what kind of natures we have for the very best institutions to work upon. But to get the best natures, can we trust, as Mr. Ball does,

to " open competition " ?   It is rather late in the day
to talk of " open competition " as a panacea for all
social ills.   Those who really wish to trust to Natural
Selection in its original form, which operates by the
extinction of the unfit, must be ready to strip the
human race of all the painfully won results of civilisation and to return, first to barbarism, and then to a
general scramble for nuts in the primeval forest—out
of which scramble, however, Natural Selection, in its
gradually ascending forms, would some day build up
civilised society again.   Open competition might
give results of some value if every one were to start
fair, run on his own legs and carry equal weight ; but
open competition between one man in a sack with a
bundle on his shoulders, another on a good horse,
and a third in an express train is a farce, and a somewhat cruel one, when the race is being run for dear
life.   Yet that is what our would-be evolutionary
politicians seriously propose ; and think themselves
" scientific " all the while !   Natural Selection must
mean something else than this before we apply it in
practical politics.

On the other hand, for Artificial Selection (which
Mr. Ball suggests as an alternative) a great deal may
be said : but the person who says it must be prepared
to be laughed at, even if he escapes the experience of
seeing "respectable persons taking off their coats and
making for him with anything that comes handy."

D. G. R.

December, 1890.

CONTENTS.

		PAGE
PREFACE	.	iii

DARWINISM AND POLITICS.

§ 1. "The Struggle for Existence" in Malthus and Darwin : How the idea is applied to Politics : Is the Struggle "beneficent?" 1

§ 2. The Evolution Theory as applied to Human Society by Darwin, Strauss, Mr. H. Spencer, Sir H. Maine, Mr. E. Clodd 6

§ 3. Ambiguity of the phrase "Survival of the Fittest:" Complexity of Social Evolution 12

§ 4. Does the doctrine of Heredity support Aristocracy? 17

§ 5. Does the Evolution Theory support *Laissez faire?* Struggle between ideas for survival : Consciousness as a factor in Evolution : Testimony of Prof. Huxley and Strauss : Ambiguity of "Nature:" Conscious "Variations" 20

§ 6. Why fix ideas in institutions? Custom—its use and abuse : Institutions and "the social factor" generally are neglected in the popular acceptation of the doctrine of Heredity : Mr. Galton's views considered : Darwin's own opinion . . 37

§ 7. The Law of Social Progress 55

§ 8. Applications :
    (1) The Labour Question 58
    (2) The Position of Women 62
    (3) The Population Question 76

  PAGE

NATURAL SELECTION AND THE SPIRITUAL WORLD.

§ 1. Darwinism complete and incomplete : Mr. A. R.
     Wallace's exclusive advocacy of Natural Selec-
     tion and desertion of it   87

§ 2. The Evolution of Morality and what it implies :
     Utilitarianism vindicated and corrected   .   .   96

§ 3. Intellectual Evolution : Mathematics, music, meta-
     physics, wit   107

§ 4. Conclusion : the true " spiritual world ".   .   .   114

NATURAL SELECTION AND THE HISTORY OF INSTITU-
     TIONS.

§ 1. Historian *versus* Evolutionist   119

§ 2. "Variation" in Sociology   121

§ 3. "Heredity" : "Survivals"   131

§ 4. "Struggle for Existence"   139

I.

DARWINISM AND POLITICS.

§ 1. *"THE STRUGGLE FOR EXISTENCE."*

CHARLES DARWIN himself has told us[1] that it was Malthus's *Essay on Population* which suggested to him the theory of Natural Selection. The constant tendency of population to outrun the means of subsistence and the consequent struggle for existence were ideas that only needed to be extended from human beings to the whole realm of organic nature in order to explain why certain inherited variations become fixed as the characteristics of definite types or species. Thus an economic treatise suggested the answer to the great biological problem; and it is therefore fitting that the biological formulæ should, in their turn, be applied to the explanation of social

---

[1] *Life and Letters of Charles Darwin*, I. p. 83. Cp. Letter to Haeckel, quoted by Grant Allen, *Darwin*, p. 67.

conditions. It is felt, rightly enough, that the problems of human society cannot be fairly studied, if we do not make use of all the light to be found in the scientific investigation of nature ; and the conception of the struggle for existence comes back to the explanation of human society with all the added force of its triumph in the solution of the greatest question with which natural science has hitherto success- fully dealt. Our sociologists look back with contempt on older phrases, such as "Social Contract" or "Natural Rights," and think that they have gained, not only a more accurate view of what is, but a rule available in practical ethics and politics. Evolution has become not merely a theory but a creed, not merely a conception by which to understand the universe, but a guide to direct us how to order our lives.

The phrase "struggle for existence," as it came from the pages of Malthus, had a dreary enough sound ; but, when this struggle for existence is shown to lead to the "survival of the fittest," and when it is seen to be the ex- planation of all the marvellous adaptations and of all the beauty of the living things in the world, it seems to gain a force and even a sanctity which makes it a very formidable opponent to have to reckon with in any political or ethical controversy. It is easy to see how the evolutionary watch-word can be applied. In Malthus the idea of struggle for existence was a very uncomfortable one; but, when it comes back to economics after passing through biology, it makes a very comfortable doctrine indeed for all those who are quite satisfied with things as they are. The support of scientific opinion can be plausibly claimed for the defence of the inequalities in the social organism; these inequalities, it can be urged, are only part of what exist inevitably throughout the physical world. The creed of Liberty, Equality, Fraternity can be discarded as a metaphysical fiction of the unscientific eighteenth century. The aspirations of socialism can be put aside as the foolish denial of the everlasting economic competition which is sanctioned by nature as only one phase of the general struggle for existence.

Let us suppose, for a moment, that our biological politicians are correct in their view of social evolution: they ought, at least, to cease talking to us of "the beneficent working of the

survival of the fittest," or "the beneficent
private war, which makes one man strive to
climb on the shoulders of another."[1] This talk
of "beneficence" is itself but a survival, not of
the fittest, but of the "theological" belief in a
God who wills the happiness of his creatures—
the attenuated creed of the English Deists—or
of the "metaphysical" belief in a Nature which,
if only left to itself, leads to better results than
can be secured by any interference of man.
That was the type of thinking in the days of
Rousseau and Adam Smith : and our evolutionary enthusiasts, when they talk of beneficence, are, after all, but repeating the creed of
the despised eighteenth century, or else they
are only disguising under a hypocritical phrase
the triumphant crowing of the successful fight-
ing-cock, aloft on his own dung-heap, while his
vanquished opponent slinks away battered and
bleeding. From natural selection there have
resulted wonderful adaptations, but how much
of suffering by the way, how much of horrid
cruelty in these adaptations themselves ? The
great Darwin himself speaks in a very different

[1] H. Spencer, *The Man versus the State*, p. 69 ; Maine,
Popular Government, p. 50.

tone from that of his jubilant disciples. Things do not look so clear to him He marvels at this wonderful universe, and especially at the nature of man, but " I cannot see," he says, "as plainly as others do, and as I should wish to do, evidence of design and beneficence on all sides of us. There seems to me too much misery in the world."[1]

> " If plagues or earthquakes break not Heav'n's design,
>   Why then a Borgia or a Catiline ? "

asks Pope with the contented optimism of his easy-going age. And if the fratricidal morality of the bee-hive and the fiendish cunning of the *Sphex* are to be admired, is there not a similar justification for military despotism and tyrannical cruelty, or for the ingenious device of the sweating system ?

> " We dined, as a rule, on each other.
>   What matter ? the toughest survived."[2]

This is a sufficient morality in the mesozoic epoch for the ichthyosaurus, to whom the senti-

[1] From a letter to Dr. Asa Gray, in *Life and Letters*, II. 312.

[2] May Kendall, *Dreams to Sell*, "Ballad of the Ichthyosaurus."

ment is ascribed by the poet; and it is a convenient morality for some human animals in
London to-day.   Admirable, doubtless—this
scheme of salvation for the elect by the damna-
tion of the vast majority; but, pray, do not let
us hear anything more about its "beneficence."

§ 2. *THE EVOLUTION THEORY APPLIED TO HUMAN SOCIETY.*

I am not speaking at random about these
ethical applications of the conception of struggle
for existence.   Darwin himself, as always, is
most cautious and guarded in his reference to
anything that lies outside his own special sphere
of observation.   He looks forward to the
elimination of the lower races by the higher
civilised races throughout the world.[1]   He
points out how "a struggle for existence consequent on his rapid multiplication," has advanced man to his present high condition;
"and, if he is to advance still higher, it is to be
feared that he must remain subject to a severe
struggle.   Otherwise he would sink into indo-
lence, and the more gifted men would not be
more successful in the battle of life than the

[1] *Life and Letters*, I. 316.

less gifted."[1] This, doubtless, includes the old objection which Aristotle brought against Plato's communism, that man needs a stimulus to exertion and industry. But there is no jubilation, no exaltation of a natural law into an ethical ideal. And let us note how Darwin modifies this very statement in the words that follow :—

"Important as the struggle for existence has been and even still is, yet as far as the highest part of man's nature is concerned there are other agencies more important. For the moral qualities are advanced, either directly or indirectly, much more through the effects of habit, the reasoning powers, instruction, religion, etc., than through natural selection; though to this latter agency may be safely attributed the social instincts which afforded the basis for the development of the moral sense."

Darwin disclaims the connexion, which had been alleged in Germany, between the doctrine of natural selection and socialism.[2] He sees clearly enough that his theory gives a *primâ facie* support not to socialism, but to industrial competition. Yet he is amused at the idea of *The Origin of Species* having turned Sir Joseph

[1] *Descent of Man*, p. 618.
[2] *Life and Letters*, III. 237.

Hooker into "a jolly old Tory." [1] "Primogeniture," he says, " is dreadfully opposed to selection : suppose the first-born bull was necessarily
made by each farmer the begetter of his stock!"
Still, he admits that English peers have an advantage in the selection of "beautiful and charm-
ing women out of the lower ranks," and thus
get some benefit from the principle.   In answer-
ing Mr. Galton's questions, Darwin describes
his own politics as " Liberal or Radical : " [2] and
this was in 1873, by which time Radicalism
was no longer bound to out-and-out *laissez
faire.*

Evolution, as applied to the whole of the
universe, means a great deal more than the
principle of natural selection.   In the wider
sense it is professedly applied to the guidance
of life by Strauss in his famous book, *The Old
Faith and the New*, where military conquest
and social inequalities are expressly defended
as right, because natural ; and nothing but contempt is reserved for those who venture to
hope for the abolition of war, who look beyond
the limits of the nation or who dream of a

---

[1] *Life and Letters*, II. 385.
[2] *Ib.* III. 178.

better social order.[1] It might be objected that
in these passages we do not hear the voice of
German science and philosophy, but of that re-
actionary military spirit which has infected the
new German nation; and I think it could be
shown that such sentiments are inconsistent
with admissions that Strauss himself makes,
although he and most German *savants* with
him believe that they are a necessary conse-
quence of the Evolutionist creed.

Let us turn, however, to our English philosopher who is always protesting against everything that can on any pretext be ascribed to
the revived militancy of the present day. In
the name of Evolution and on behalf of the
survival of the fittest Mr. Herbert Spencer
cries out against " The Sins of Legislators " in
interfering with the beneficent operation of the
pitiless discipline which kills off the unsuccessful members of society, and against " The Coming Slavery," which he supposes would result
from socialistic attempts to diminish the misery
of the world.[2] Now, just as in Strauss's case

---

[1] See esp. secs. 78, 79, 82, 83, 84 in German (ed. 8.
1875) = secs. 74, 75, 78, 79, 80 in Eng. Tr. (ed. 3. 1874).
[2] See *The Man v. the State*, esp. the two essays named.

the military spirit, so in Spencer's the old-
fashioned individualistic radicalism of his early
days might be assigned as the true source of
such opinions ; but there can be no doubt that
the formulæ of Evolution do supply an apparent justification to the defenders of unrestricted
laissez faire and to the champions, more or less
consistent and thorough-going, of existing inequalities of race, class and sex, and a plausible
weapon of attack against those who look to
something better than slavery or competition
as the basis of human society. Thus Spencer
rejoices over the Liberty and Property Defence
League, " largely consisting of Conservatives,"[1]
and the late Sir Henry Maine in the congenial
pages of the *Quarterly Review*[2] rejoiced over
Mr. Herbert Spencer and glorified "the
beneficent private war" of economical competition, which he considered the only alternative
to "the daily task, enforced by the prison and
the scourge." "So far," he says, "as we have
any experience to teach us, we are driven to
the conclusion that every society of men must

---

[1] *The Man versus the State*, p. 17.
[2] Republished in *Popular Government*. See pp. 49, 50,
52.

adopt one system or the other, or it will pass
through penury to starvation."

Even those who are more full of hope for
the future and more full of sympathy for human
beings, are apt to adopt a similar mode of
speaking. Thus, in his interesting little book,
The Story of Creation, Mr. Edward Clodd,
though he looks forward to "a goal, where
might shall be subdued by right," yet speaks
as follows :—

"When the weeding process has done its utmost, there
remains a sharp struggle for life between the survivors.
Man's normal state is therefore one of conflict; further
back than we can trace, it impelled the defenceless bipeds
from whom he sprang to unity, and the more so because of
their relative inferiority in physique to many other animals.
The range of that unity continued narrow long after he had
gained lordship over the brute ; outside the small combinations for securing the primal needs of life the struggle
was ferocious, and, under one form or another, rages along
the line to this day. 'There is no discharge in that war.'
It may change its tactics and its weapons : among advanced
nations the military method may be more or less superseded
by the industrial, a man may be mercilessly starved instead
of being mercilessly slain ; but be it war of camp or mar-
kets, the ultimate appeal is to force of brain or muscle, and
the hardiest or craftiest win. In some respects the struggle
is waged more fiercely than in olden times, while it is un-
redeemed by any element of chivalry." (pp. 211, 212.)

It is thus of the extremest practical importance to see what is the real bearing of Evolution on social problems. We must examine
the relation between biological laws and social
faiths and hopes, if we would make our opinions
self - consistent ;   and self - consistency is the
negative test of truth.   Such an examination is
especially incumbent on those who profess to
keep their minds open to all that science can
teach, and at the same time to have at heart
the cause of social reformation.   We ought to
have a reason for the faith that is in us.   To
test our scattered opinions and beliefs by bringing them together is the main function of a
sound philosophy.

§ 3. *"SURVIVAL OF THE FITTEST."*

The phrase "survival of the fittest" is very
apt to mislead, for it suggests the fittest or best
in every sense or in the highest sense, whereas
it only means, as Prof. Huxley has pointed out,
those " best fitted to cope with their circumstances "[1] in order to survive and transmit

[1] Art. on "The Struggle for Existence," in *Nineteenth
Century* for Feb., 1888, p. 165.

offspring. Now when we come to consider
society, we have to deal with a very complex
set of phenomena, and what is fittest in one
aspect may not be fittest in another. But
natural selection implies no further morality
than " Nothing succeeds like success." If the
struggle for food and mates be carried on on its
lowest terms, the strongest and the strongest
only would be selected. But cunning can do a
great deal against strength. Now we cannot
be sure that a good combination of strength
and cunning will be selected : strength in some
cases, cunning in others—this is what we find
if we compare different species of animals and
different races of men. Again, the strongest
and largest and in many ways finest animals
are not necessarily those most capable of adapt-
ing themselves to changed circumstances. The
insignificant may more easily find food and
escape enemies. We cannot be sure that
Evolution will always lead to what we should
regard as the greatest perfection of any species.
Degeneration enters in as well as progress.
The latest theory about the Aryan race makes
it come from the north of Europe, conquer the
feebler races of the south, and, having proved

its fitness in this way, prove its unfitness in
another by being less capable of surviving in a
warm climate than they; so that an Aryan
language may be spoken, where there remains
little or no Aryan blood.[1]   Are we entitled to
maintain, with regard to human races and
human individuals, that the fittest always survive, except in the sense in which the proposi-
tion is the truism, that those survive who are
most capable of surviving?

Further, we must emphasize the fact that the
struggle goes on not merely between individual
and individual, but between race and race.
The struggle among plants and the lower
animals is mainly between members of the
same species; and the individual competition
between human beings, which is so much
admired by Mr. Herbert Spencer, is of this
primitive kind. When we come to the struggle
between kinds, it is to be noticed that it is
fiercest between allied kinds; and so, as has
been pointed out, the economic struggle between Great Britain and the United States is
fiercer than elsewhere between nations. But,

<hr />

[1] See Art. by Prof. Rhys on "Race Theories and European Politics," in *New Princeton Review*, Jan., 1888.

so soon as we pass to the struggle between
race and race, we find new elements coming in.
The race which is fittest to survive, *i.e.* most
capable of surviving, will survive ; but it does
not therefore follow that the individuals thereby preserved will be fittest, either in the sense
of being those who in a struggle between
individual and individual would have survived,
or in the sense of being those whom we should
regard as the finest specimens of their kind.
A race or a nation may succeed by crushing
out the chances of the great majority of its
individual members. The cruel polity of the
bees, the slave-holding propensities of certain
species of ants have their analogues in human
societies. The success of Sparta in the Hellenic world was obtained at the cost of a frightful oppression of her subject classes and with
the result that Sparta never produced one
really great man. How much more does the
world owe to Athens which failed, than to
Sparta which succeeded in the physical struggle
for existence ?

But human beings are not merely, like plants
and animals, grouped into natural species or
varieties. They have come to group them-

selves in very various ways. Thus an individual may, conceivably, belong by descent to one group, by political allegiance to another, by language, and all that language carries with it of tradition and culture, to a third, by religion to a fourth, by occupation to a fifth— though in most cases two or more of these will coincide. Now between each of these groups and similar groups there are, as the doctrine of Evolution teaches us if we need to be taught, struggles constantly proceeding. Race struggles with race, nation with nation, language with language, religion with religion, and social castes based on occupation and on economic *status* struggle with one another for pre-eminence, apart from the struggle going on between individuals and groups of individuals within each of them. Now, if in each of these cases the struggle were not complicated by the other struggles, we might contentedly assert that natural selection leads to the fittest always succeeding. But a defeated and subject race may impose its language, its civilisation, or its religion upon its conquerors ; and the apparent failure of a race or a nation does not entitle us at once to pronounce it inferior or less fit, because its failure in warfare may be the prelude to a greater and more lasting success in peace.

§ 4. *DOES THE DOCTRINE OF HEREDITY SUPPORT ARISTOCRACY?*

On the other hand, it is easy to see how the pre-eminence of a caste, based either on race or on occupation, may be maintained at the cost of the physical and intellectual advance of its members. Where noble may marry only noble and where marriages are " arranged," as the phrase runs (more truthful than most of those current in the fashionable world), the interests of the health and of the intelligence of the race may be sacrificed to the maintenance of a closely coherent class with large estates and social predominance. Such a type of nobility will in the long run inevitably lose power owing to its own internal decay through continued intermarriage and lack of new blood. Yet superficially plausible arguments from the doctrine of heredity are occasionally brought forward in its favour. The democrat is often told that he is very unscientific ; but the evolutionist, who points to the aristocratic preferences of history, errs greatly if he thinks the

C

undoubted pre-eminence of a few great individuals and even of a few famous families any
sound argument in favour of a hereditary
aristocratic caste.   Darwin, as we have already
seen, admits that the nobility in this country
have a certain advantage in being able to
select their wives more freely than most other
men : yet, allowing their superiority in this
matter to the nobilities of other countries and
rejoicing that the institution of the peerage
has saved us from the worse calamity of a
" nobility " in the proper sense, we may be
permitted to regret that these highly privileged
persons, the peers and the peers' eldest sons,
do not always think sufficiently of their responsibility to the future in the selection of
their mates.   Darwin, as we have also seen,
inveighs against the folly of primogeniture : so
that, after all, even the English nobility do
not get much countenance from the theory of
natural selection.   It is strange to find the
doctrine of heredity invoked by the defenders
of the House of Lords : one would suspect
that they have never looked into Mr. Galton's
interesting book.   It is instructive to notice
the way in which half-understood scientific

theories are misapplied to practical matters.
Mr. Galton declares most emphatically that he
looks upon the peerage "as a disastrous institution, owing to its destructive effects on our
valuable races." If an eminent man is elevated
to the House of Lords, his eldest son is
tempted to marry a wealthy heiress, in order
to keep up the show required of a hereditary
legislator ; but wealthy heiresses usually tend
to be sterile, being the last representatives of
dwindling families. On the other hand, owing
to the custom of primogeniture, the younger
sons are induced to remain unmarried : and
thus the peerage appears to be an ingenious
device for hindering the propagation of talent.[1]
Further Mr. Galton shows clearly enough the
absurdity of expecting to find ability transmitted through a long line of descent : the
older a man's family, therefore, the less likely
is he to have inherited any of the ability of its
founder. I suppose there is still a pious Conservative superstition that " our old nobility "
can boast of its " Norman blood "—a belief
which a critical examination of a recent copy
of the *Peerage* would do a good deal to weaken

[1] See Galton's *Hereditary Genius*, p. 140.

But even supposing the Norman blood were there, does it follow that it is now particularly worth having? " It is curious to remark," says Mr. Galton, " how unimportant to modern civilisation has become the once famous and thoroughbred looking Norman. The type of his features, which is, probably, in some degree correlated with his peculiar form of adventurous disposition, is no longer characteristic of our rulers, and is rarely found among celebrities of the present day ; it is more often met with among the undistinguished members of highly born families, and especially among the less conspicuous officers of the army." [1]   I have not yet raised the question as to what kind of characteristics can be transmitted from generation to generation and in what way : I have only tried to show that the scientific doctrine of heredity is a very treacherous ally of the defenders of aristocratic privilege.

§ 5. *DOES THE EVOLUTION THEORY SUPPORT*
" LAISSEZ FAIRE"?

The doctrine of Evolution gives little support to the aristocratic Conservative.   It may seem

[1] *Hereditary Genius*, p. 348.

to give more to the "*laissez faire*" Radical. The evolutionist politician is more likely to adopt the view that in the interests of the race we ought to remove every artificial restriction on the operation of natural and sexual selection. But the difficulty is—where are we to find a line between "natural" and "artificial," if all the phenomena of society are, as the evolutionist is bound to hold, subject to the same laws of nature? If we are content to remove only some artificial restrictions, on what principle can we justify ourselves? If we are to remove every artificial restriction that hampers the struggle for existence, are we not going back to Rousseau's "State of Nature," the primitive, uncivilised, pre-social condition of mankind? If we expect the "State of Nature" to be better than the present condition, which is one of at least mitigated or inconsistent anarchy, are we not falling back into the "metaphysical" conception of Nature and ignoring the scientific conception of society? The "State of Nature," *i.e.* the unsocial state, is more correctly described by Hobbes as "the war of all against all." On the other hand, when we find the more tender-hearted preacher of evolutionist morality point-

ing out that, though the physical well-being of
the race may have suffered through the mitigation of the primitive struggle and the consequent preservation of weaklings, we have
gained some intellectual advance through the
occasional chance of a Newton and a moral
advance through the cultivation of sympathy
and tenderness,[1] in such a position is there not
some inconsistency, some sacrifice of natural
selection in favour of human selection consciously or half-consciously directed to other
ends than those of mere nature ?   Our attention
is thus called to another factor in that universal
strife which is the story of the universe.   So
soon as a sufficient social development and a
sufficiently advanced type of language make it
possible, there begins a competition between
ideas.   The age of conflict is, in Bagehot's
phrase,[2] succeeded by " the age of discussion,"
and the ideas, which rise in the minds of men
with the same tendency to variation that we find
throughout nature, compete with one another
for sustenance and support.   The conception of
natural selection may be applied here also to

[1] E. Clodd, *Story of Creation,* p. 211.
[2] *Physics and Politics.*

explain how certain ideas come to obtain that relatively fixed and definite character which belongs, for instance, to the moral principles currently accepted within a community at any given time. Thus such ideas as patriotism, respect of human life as such, self-control in regard to the bodily appetites, have won their way so as to become factors in the struggle and to conflict with the operation of natural selection as this prevails among the mere animals. Why then may not such ideas as Equality and Fraternity claim to have a fair chance in the struggle for existence? If they can win possession of more and more minds in the world, they will become actual influences on conduct and will from being mere ideals tend to bring about their own realisation,[1] "Opinions," said Lord Palmerston, "are stronger than armies." One of the first conditions of any institution being altered is that people should come to imagine it as altered. The great difficulty of the reformer is to get people to exert their imagination to that extent.

Now what does all this amount to except to

[1] Cp. Fouillée, *La Science Sociale Contemporaine*, p xii., etc.

a recognition of the difference introduced into
natural evolution by the appearance of *consciousness?*   I shall not now attempt to work out all
the philosophical implications involved in this
recognition of consciousness : nor, in order to
show how through consciousness man becomes
free from the tyranny of nature, shall I quote
the words of any one whose evidence might be
suspected because he might be called a mere
metaphysician.   I shall quote the words of a
witness whom no scientific man would reject—
Professor Huxley :—

"Society, like art, is a part of nature.   But it is convenient
to distinguish those parts of nature in which man plays the
part of immediate cause as something apart ; and, therefore,
society, like art, is usefully to be considered as distinct from
nature.   It is the more desirable, and even necessary, to
make this distinction, since society differs from nature in
having a definite moral object ; whence it comes about that
the course shaped by the ethical man—the member of society
or citizen—necessarily runs counter to that which the non-
ethical man—the primitive savage, or man as a mere member
of the animal kingdom—tends to adopt.   The latter fights
out the struggle for existence to the bitter end, like any
other animal ; the former devotes his best energies to the
object of setting limits to the struggle.

.   .   .   .   .   .

"The history of civilisation—that is of society—is the
record of the attempts which the human race has made to

escape from this position [*i.e.* the struggle for existence in which those who were best fitted to cope with their circumstances, but not the best in any other sense, survived]. The first men who substituted the state of mutual peace for that of mutual war, whatever the motive which impelled them to take that step, created society. But in establishing peace, they obviously put a limit upon the struggle for existence. Between the members of that society, at any rate, it was not to be pursued *à outrance*. And of all the successive shapes which society has taken, that most nearly approaches perfection in which war of individual against individual is most strictly limited."[1]

Professor Huxley then goes on to show how the struggle for existence appears in a new form through the zealous fulfilment of what we are told was the first commandment given to man— "Be fruitful and multiply." But, instead of arguing, as before, that the further history of civilisation must consist in putting a limit to this new economic struggle, he avoids drawing any such inference, and very lamely concludes that we must establish technical schools. These are most desirable and necessary institutions, but they might fulfil some better purpose than what he proposes—which is simply to sharpen our claws that we may fight our neighbours

---

[1] Art. "The Struggle for Existence," in *Nineteenth Century*, Feb., 1888, pp. 165, 166.

the more fiercely and destroy them the more successfully. Let us be grateful, however, to Professor Huxley for the scientific conclusions which he has drawn. As practical premises they will serve us for a wider syllogism than he ventures to construct. It is the same with Strauss. In spite of his excessive conservatism in practical matters, this is the way in which he formulates in general terms the " Rule of Life " :—

"Ever remember that thou art human, not merely a natural production ; ever remember that all others are human also, and, with all individual differences, the same as thou, having the same needs and claims as thyself : this is the sum and substance of morality."

" In man Nature endeavoured not merely to exalt, but to transcend herself. He must not therefore be merely an animal repeated ; he must be something more, something better."

"Man not only can and should know Nature, but rule both external Nature, so far as his powers admit, and the natural within himself."[1]

It is unnecessary here to raise the question how consciousness makes its appearance. It is enough that human beings are not only engaged

[1] *The Old Faith and the New.* Eng. Transl. ii. pp. 54, 57, 58 (secs. 70, 71 = secs. 74, 75 in German edit. 1875).

in the struggle for existence, but *know* that they
are so engaged, are capable of looking round
on what they are doing, of reflecting, of com-
paring results and considering some good, some
bad, some to be desired and others to be
avoided.   If we distinguish — as Professor
Huxley says it is convenient to do—between
man and nature, then it is of extreme importance to us to discover the natural laws which
operate in society, but it does not follow that
we owe them any allegiance.   They are " laws "
simply in the sense of being generalisations
from experience of facts or hypotheses by
which we find it possible to make the facts more
intelligible to ourselves : and it is the merest
ambiguity of language that leads to the argument that what can be called " an economic
law " has any claim upon our reverence.   It may
tell us something convenient or something inconvenient ; but of itself it is, like nature,
absolutely non-moral.

On the other hand, if we use Nature (with
a very big N) to include *all* that goes on in
human society, human institutions and human
ideas must be included in this conception of
Nature : else the scientific sociologist is assum-

ing a supernatural, or infranatural, region outside human society. Governments are natural
products, and it is inconsistent in Mr. Herbert
Spencer, while telling us that the maxim " Con-
stitutions are not made but grow " has become
a truism, to go on to blame governments simply
because they " interfere" with natural laws.
Why, such " interferences " would on his own
principles amount to a miracle! The real and
significant distinction is not that between
" State-interference" and " *laissez faire*," but
between intelligent and scientific, *i.e.* systematic and far-sighted State-action on the one
side and that peddling kind of playing at an
occasional and condescending providence in
small matters, which is often much worse than
doing nothing at all. The State which "pro-
tects" a few industries and doles out its alms
to a multitude of paupers is only yet half conscious of its functions and may be doing unmitigated evil, except in so far as it is performing
some interesting but rather cruel experiments
for the benefit of sociological students. " Protection " and a bad poor-law (*i.e.* any mode of
relief which breeds pauperism instead of dimin-
ishing it) are just the kinds of State-action which

have brought all State-action into disrepute and make the arguments against it plausible. There are, however, many cases where the arguments against a partial State-action cease to hold against the same action if made more thoroughgoing : *e.g.* giving free education to some children may be objected to as pauperising ; free education as the right of all would make none paupers. Yet even a partial State-action may often be welcomed, as a recognition that the State has duties towards its weaker members, however inefficiently it may discharge them.

The capacity for thinking constitutes man's freedom. It is by thinking alone that he can rise above the position of nature's slave. This does not amount to asserting the foolish dogma of arbitrary "free will"—as if every human being were always equally capable of choosing between any given course and its opposite—a dogma which is not only foolish, but mischievous, for it leads to the neglect of the way in which individual characters depend on their environment, and to the consequent neglect of the moral importance of political and social institutions. Ideas are themselves the outcome

of institutions; and yet they constitute a factor
that must be taken account of, if we are to
form an adequate conception of social evolution.

What is effected by conscious effort is not
necessarily in antagonism to what was going on
in the unconscious stage. More often it is a
continuation, an extension, an acceleration of a
process already begun. In the higher organisms, even apart from consciousness, there is, at
least according to Mr. Spencer's generalisation,
less waste than in the lower. Thus the plants
that are fertilised by insects produce fewer pollen
grains than those which have no conspicuous
flowers. Those which have fruits that are attrac-
tive to birds produce fewer seeds than crypto-
gamous plants, whose germs fill the air in count-
less myriads. The great mortality of savage
life and the prevalence of infanticide are similar
instances of waste which disappear more or less
at higher stages in social evolution. It is very
easy for the historian to show how much service has been rendered to mankind by fierce
struggles, by war, civil dissension, economic
competition. But does it therefore follow that
equally good ends can never be attained at less

cost ?   Strauss insists that it is as impossible
to abolish war, as to abolish thunder-storms.
To argue thus is to proceed like certain Indians
who are said to cut down the fruit tree when
they wish to pluck the fruit, or like Charles
Lamb's Chinaman, who burnt down his house
every time he wanted to enjoy the luxury of
roast pig.   Are we to have so much more faith
in the blind passions of human nature than in
what can be done by conscious effort ?   With
these blind passions we must reckon, as with
other forces in nature : but there is no reason
why we should accord to them any special
prestige, simply because they are natural.
They are to be used or to be defeated according as our thinking decides.

War is "natural" only in the sense of being
the primitive form of the struggle between races
and nations, not in the sense of something which
ought to be.   It has indeed contributed greatly
to nation-making and to the development of
the primitive virtues of courage and fidelity.
Those tribes that were the bravest and the
most coherent have been the most successful in
the struggle for existence, and so these virtues
have come to receive special respect.   But let

us notice with what limitations—courage was
limited to the courage shown in the battle-field,
fidelity was limited to fidelity towards one's
own tribe. When reflection begins, and when
imagination is developed, the sphere of courage
and fidelity comes to be extended, at least in
the minds of some of the more reflective and
sympathetic individuals. It is precisely in this
way that moral ideas, which are the product
of social evolution, come to be capable of
advance and progress. Customs—and customs
are laws in their primitive form—are habits regarded as right, because, having been adopted,
they have proved conducive to the welfare
and success of the tribe or nation ; but customs
tend to survive long after the circumstances
which called them into being have changed.
If they become very hurtful, the people maintaining them will in the long run suffer in the
struggle with nature or with other nations
which have better customs, *i.e.* customs more
favourable to success; but it is a gain to a people
if its more far-sighted members discern the hurt-
fulness of a custom in time, and persuade or
force their fellows to discard it before it is too
late. This is in all ages the function of the

political, religious, or social reformer—to save
his people from destruction or decay by induc-
ing them to change a custom which, however
beneficial once, and in some respects, has now
become mischievous. Such attempts imply no
contradiction to the principle of modification by
natural selection, but are themselves an illustration of it. / Suppose an animal, whose ancestors
lived on the land, takes to the water (or *vice
versâ*) because circumstances have changed, or
in order to escape from excessive competition ;
it may succeed better. When Themistocles
made the Athenians into a naval power, this
change was a quite analogous phenomenon.
The difference is, that what Darwin called (confessedly as a mode of expressing ignorance)
the "spontaneous" variation in the habits of
the animal is supplanted by the deliberate adoption of a new habit among human beings.

Now among all the more advanced societies
we find this conscious, deliberate adaptation
supplanting the unconscious and spontaneous,
though in the beginnings of the most successful
institutions there is generally a very large
element of unconsciousness in the procedure.
Thus the great discovery of representative

government, which constitutes the chief difference between ancient and modern politics,
which has made it possible for democracy to
exist without slavery, and which has made it
possible for large states to possess free institutions, came about mainly because Englishmen
felt it inconvenient to attend personally when
the King wished to obtain money : an irksome
duty was readily transferred to others.[1]   But
representative government, as maintained by
civil war in the seventeenth century, and representative government as imitated in all the
most advanced nations of the world, is something consciously and deliberately chosen.   It
is a further and more complex application of
the convenient principle of " counting heads to
save the trouble of breaking them."   Federa-
tion, in its modern sense,[2] is a still further and
still more complex application of the same
principle, though Strauss, with the prejudices
of a German monarchist, thinks a federal state

[1] See Hearn, *Government of England*, 2nd Edit. pp. 466 ff.
[2] I add this qualification, because the Federations of
ancient history appear not to have recognised, except in
rudimentary form, the principle of representation, and thus
belonged to a lower, not a higher, type of society than the
city-state.

inferior to a nation. We may feel dissatisfied
enough with what representative institutions
still are, even at their best and when honestly
worked; but we should be indulging in a
foolish paradox if we did not see that any such
institutions are better than their absence,
because of the possibilities they contain. Yet
could any political thinker of the ancient world
have believed such institutions possible?
Would he have believed it possible for free
citizens to delegate their functions, even for
a time, without surrendering their democratic
freedom?[1] One can see in Strauss's book how
little understanding the cultured German may
still have of this great condition of political
advance.[2]

Does not the introduction of representative
government, which has solved and will solve

---

[1] In enumerating the different kinds of oligarchy, Aristotle
gives what is practically a definition of representative
government (*Pol.* iv. 14 § 8, 1298 *a* 40); but this is merely
put forward as a logical possibility. At least he gives no
example, and this slight naming is the clearest proof of the
absence of the *idea* from the mind of the greatest political
thinker of antiquity.

[2] *The Old Faith and the New*, sec. 81 (German ed. 1875)
= sec. 77 Eng. Tr.

many problems, however many it leaves
unsolved, hold out the promise that similar
good may be done by the substitution of some
more intelligent methods for military and industrial competition? International arbitration
and economic co-operation are as yet small
beginnings, but not smaller than the first germs
of representative government. So far as we
have yet got, neither arbitration nor co-operation have done for society what their advocates hoped, but they may be the first
" variations," which, if they prove their fitness,
will bring into being a new species of civilised
society.

Mr. Herbert Spencer considers that there
are only two main types of society, the militant
and the industrial: and in industrialism he com-
prehends an absolute system of *laissez faire*,
the extreme of individualism. It is strange
that he should not see that the economic
struggle is only a phase of the oldest form of
struggle for existence—the struggle between
individuals for subsistence, and that it therefore
belongs to a lower type than the struggles
between organised communities, where a strict
organisation mitigates the internal strife. It is

difficult to see whence Mr. Spencer and his followers derive their ardent faith in a beneficent result from this struggle, unless it be, as already suggested, from an inconsistent survival of the old theological optimism or the metaphysical idea of Nature.

§ 6. *IDEAS AND INSTITUTIONS.—THE "SOCIAL FACTOR."*

But, it might be objected, the economic struggle is not unmitigated, for industrial competition is carried on amongst enlightened and educated people, who will consider one another and develop their altruistic tendencies, though not in excess. Yet so fearful is Mr. Spencer of the interference of the State with his social aggregate of warring atoms, that he will not hear of any education except what each family provides for its own members—a return to the patriarchal or "Cyclopic" type of society—or what can be provided by free competition between private teachers, who will run the educational business on strict commercial principles. Thus I am afraid the educational influences to which he looks will not operate rapidly. But why, it will be said, not trust to

the spread of kindlier feelings among individuals
to mitigate the harshness of inevitable natural
laws ? Why bring in the ponderous machinery
of legislation ? Why crystallise customs into
codes, voluntary associations into definite
political institutions ?

I have already referred to the mischief and
danger that may arise from customs which have
outlived their use ; but fixed customs, as Bagehot has so admirably pointed out,[1] are essential
in keeping society together, and, as all scientific
students of ethics have come to see, morality is
dependent upon institutions.   We may have to
fight against custom to get a hearing for new
ideas ; but we must make use of custom to get
them realised.   Ideas can only be productive
of their full benefit, if they are fixed in institutions.   We cannot build up anything on a mere
shifting basis of opinion.   This principle is
equally applicable to the removal of old wrongs
and to the introduction of new rights.   Many
kindly and enlightened persons here and there
felt the evil of slavery, but their views were
mere isolated private opinions till slavery was
abolished by legal enactment in one country

[1] *Physics and Politics,* p. 25 ff.

after another throughout the civilised world. Highly respectable and pious people in the last century had no objection even to the slave-trade. Now that slavery has been officially buried, it has not many friends left to shed tears over its grave. Certain eccentric individuals were disposed to favour religious toleration in the sixteenth and seventeenth centuries. But even those who, being inclined to heresy themselves, like John Milton and John Locke, extended the bounds of liberty pretty far, had very distinct limits beyond which they would not go. There is always the risk of an outburst of the persecuting spirit, even in communities that are not as a rule fiercely fanatical. Hence a great step is gained when in any country it is expressly and officially declared that distinctions of creed shall make no difference in the rights of citizens. It is often argued that the possession of the suffrage is of very infinitesimal value to the poor man and will do very little good to the poor woman when she gets it. What is a vote to those who are in want of bread? A vote is not merely an occasional and indirect means of exerting a small fraction of political influence, but, what is

much more important, it is a stamp of full
citizenship, of dignity and of responsibility. It
is a distinct mark that the possessors of it can
no longer be systematically ignored by governments and can no longer shirk the duty of
thinking about public and common interests.
The slaves of a kindly master, the subjects of
a kindly tyrant or ruling caste may be very
comfortable animals : but the master or tyrant
may become unkindly or impotent, and the
poor wretches who have been dependent on
him suffer without being able to help themselves. It is always much easier to ignore an
unuttered or feebly uttered claim than to revoke
a right once granted. The same remark applies to the acquisition of representative institutions by a country or a locality : it marks a
step gained which is not likely to be lost. Few
persons, at least in this country, care so very
much for the abstract advantage of a republic
over a monarchy. A nominal republic may be
less democratic than a nominal monarchy :
and to change a state into a republic might in
some cases be grasping the shadow and letting
the substance go. But a republic has at least
this advantage, that it does not call the

sovereign power by the name of a person or dynasty, but proclaims it before all the world "the commonwealth." "*Noblesse oblige :*" and a republic sets up a higher standard of political morality and thus deserves to be more harshly judged, if it falls short even of a monarchy and imitates in any way the follies and vices that are hardly avoidable where there is a royal court.

Another reason why ideas should be embodied in institutions, is that institutions exert so great an influence upon human character— an influence sometimes ignored on professedly scientific grounds. Perhaps the most popularly accepted part of the evolution theory is the doctrine of heredity ; but it may be questioned how far the popular view, nay, even the view of many who have been trained in science, is not in reality the survival of a very ancient superstition,[1] the belief in an inherited family destiny, a belief which was the natural product of a time when the family or tribe was the social and

---

[1] In a notice of this essay in *Mind*, vol. xiv. p. 291, it is actually alleged that I say that "the doctrine of heredity may be nothing more than the survival of a very ancient superstition !" I say nothing of the kind. I suggest that *the popular view* of heredity may be a *mixture* of science and superstition.

moral unit. Plato, in the *Laws*,[1] professes to
regard robbers of temples as persons suffering
from an incurable malady, "a madness be-
gotten in a man from ancient and unexpiated
crimes of his race, destroying him when his
time is come." Aristotle uses the idea to make
a quiet professorial joke, when he is speaking
about certain abnormal moral tendencies : he
tells of the man who excused himself for beating
his father by saying that it was an inherited
practice in his family for the son to beat the
father, and of another family in which the sons
used to drag their father to the door but no
further.[2] There is indeed a singular fascination,
horrible at times as it may be, in the idea that
the experiences of ancestors survive as the
feelings of the descendants; but a great part
of the prevalent opinion about heredity seems
to be only mythology or fiction masquerading
as science. Of course one who is not a
biologist has no right to a private opinion in
a biological controversy. But one must feel a
keen interest in the discussion at present going
on, as to whether acquired characteristics are
transmitted or not. The negative opinion

[1] ix. 854.   [2] *Eth. Nic.* vii. 6 § 2.

appears to be on the increase, *i.e.* the Lamarckian doctrine is tending to disappear from the
evolution theory and the Darwinian principle
of natural selection acting upon "spontaneous"
variations is coming to be accepted as the sole
factor in organic evolution.[1] "Use and disuse"
seem at first sight so much easier to understand
than "natural selection," that it will probably
be some time before they lose their hold on the
imagination. The temptation undoubtedly is
to discuss the question at once in its application to human beings, but it can be more safely
discussed with regard to the lower animals,
both because the opportunities of experiment
are better and because there is less risk of bias
in forming inferences. In the case of human
beings it is so very difficult to distinguish what
is due to inheritance in the restricted sense of
race-influence from what is due to imitation,
early training, etc., which constitute inheritance
certainly—but in a wider and a sociological, not
a merely biological, sense. When people point
to the remarkable way in which children re-
semble their parents, they are apt to forget that
children as a rule are not merely the children

---

[1] See below, pp. 87, 88.

of their parents, but spend all their earliest years with their parents.   Even where a parent is dead, the child is told of his or her habits and ways of thought, and unconscious imitation of a father or mother, whose memory is regarded as something sacred, may account for a great deal.   Mr. Galton, in his work on *Hereditary Genius*, admits that his investigations altogether suffer from the defect that there is so great a "lack of reliable information" about the peculiarities of females (p. 63). We shall have to wait till public careers are more abundantly open to women before much can be learnt from family pedigrees.   It is certainly striking that, in the two sets of cases where Mr. Galton considers the maternal influence to be strong, viz., in the case of scientific men and in the case of pious divines (pp. 196, 276), his own explanation turns upon influence in early years and not upon mere birth. The clever mother encourages and does not discourage the inquiring child; the pious mother, if she manages to influence her son at all, directs all his thoughts and emotions into one channel.   It seems very doubtful whether, except in fairy tales or romances, the child brought up away from its parents and in complete ignorance of them (for this also is essential to a fair experiment) would present any of their moral characteristics in a definite form. May we say that a certain amount of psychical energy is inherited, but the direction it takes is mostly determined by circumstances? — though we must admit that it may be of a kind which more readily takes to certain occupations than to others. Individuals start with inherited tendencies or capacities (φυσικαὶ δυνάμεις, ὁρμαί), not with fully formed habits (ἀφωρισμέναι ἕξεις). An energetic or an apathetic temperament, a cool or a nervous temperament is transmitted ; but it seems very doubtful how far mere inheritance goes beyond that, apart from the external influences in early life, which generally act along with it. As we see so often, the son of people who have pushed themselves up in the world and made their fortune, may inherit the energy of his ancestors but not their busi· ness habits, and so he may only go to the devil more vehemently than others who come of a race longer accustomed to prosperity and who get an early training in the more elegant squandering of wealth.

On this subject of heredity, though Darwin was too modest to urge his own discovery of natural selection to its full length, he is much more cautious in his statements than many who are fond of using his name. In his Autobiography, it is true, he says :—" I am inclined to agree with Francis Galton in believing that education and environment produce only a small effect on the mind of any one, and that most of our qualities are innate." [1] But in the *Descent of Man* [2] his position is much more guarded, and he seems generally to allow early influence to account for more than inheritance, in respect of virtuous habits, etc. With regard to himself he says that he owed his "humanity" to the instruction and example of his sisters. [3] His statement that "handwriting is certainly inherited" seems a very doubtful one. [4] In his

[1] *Life and Letters*, I. 22.

[2] *e.g.* pp. 122-125. On p. 123 he says :—" There is not the least inherent improbability, it seems to me, in virtuous tendencies being more or less strongly inherited." This is a very negative and cautious position.

[3] *Life and Letters*, I. 29. " I doubt indeed whether humanity is a natural or innate quality."

[4] *Descent of Man*, p. 88. He refers to *Variation of Animals and Plants under Domestication*, vol. II. p. 6. [See I. p. 449 in edition 2.]

Life of Erasmus Darwin[1] he says that his uncle
Charles Darwin " inherited stammering " from
his father, Erasmus. " With the hope of curing
him his father sent him to France, when about
eight years old, with a private tutor, thinking
that if he was not allowed to speak English for
a time, the habit of stammering might be lost ;
and it is a curious fact, that in after years, when
speaking French he never stammered." Is
not this " curious fact" an *instantia crucis* which
proves that his stammering was *not* inherited ?
If it had been, he must have stammered in
every language.

The lower down we go in the scale of animal
intelligence the more seems due to inherited
instincts : the higher we go the more is due
to imitation and to the training rendered
possible by the greater size and complexity of
the brain and necessary by the prolongation of
infancy. In the lower animals any habit which
is useful to the preservation of the species can
only be transmitted as an instinct. In the
higher animals much can be done by imitation
and instruction. Among human beings, language and social institutions make it possible to

[1] p. 80, quoted in *Life and Letters*, I. 7.

transmit experience quite independently of the
continuity of race, so that even if a family
or a race dies out altogether, its intellectual and
moral acquirements and culture are not necessarily lost to the world.   An individual or a
nation may do more for mankind by handing
on ideas and a great example than by leaving
numerous offspring.   Darwin himself fully
admits this :—

"A man who was not impelled by any deep instinctive
feeling to sacrifice his life for the good of others, yet was
roused to such action by a sense of glory, would by his
example excite the same wish for glory in other men, and
would strengthen by exercise the noble feeling of admiration.   He might thus do far more good to his tribe than by
begetting offspring with a tendency to inherit his own high
character."   (*Descent of Man*, p. 132.)
"Great lawgivers, the founders of beneficent religions,
great philosophers and discoverers in science, aid the progress of mankind in a far higher degree by their works than
by leaving a numerous progeny."   (*ib.* p. 136.)

What Darwin says here of the greatest of men
is also in a less degree true of men generally.
Most certainly we inherit from those who have
gone before us : but the "inheritance" in
any advanced civilisation is far more in the
intellectual and moral environment—in the

spiritual air we breathe, than in the blood that runs in our veins.[1]

Mr. Galton's investigations on heredity do not appear to commit him to the Lamarckian or Spencerian view that *acquired* intellectual or moral characteristics are inherited; and, as we have already seen, he in some cases fully recognises how much the environment of the individual in early years affects his course in life. But it cannot be denied that Mr. Galton *seems* to lend countenance to a sort of fatalism about the influence of race, and to a too contented acquiescence in existing social arrangements. I say advisedly "seems," because I do not think Mr. Galton's book is quite as comforting to the opponents of change, if they come to read it carefully, instead of merely claiming its authority on their side. Let us consider a few passages in detail. " It is in the most un-qualified manner that I object to pretensions of natural equality. . . . I acknowledge freely the great power of education and social influences in developing the active powers of

---

[1] Cp. Lewes, *The Study of Psychology*, pp. 78–80, where it is urged that the operation of " the social factor" constitutes the difference between man and the lower animals.

the mind, just as I acknowledge the effect of
use in developing the muscles of a blacksmith's
arm, and no further." There is a definite
limit to the muscular [and intellectual] power
of every man, which he cannot by any education or exertion over-pass.[1] If this is the
dictum of science, it might seem for a moment
to deal a fatal blow to the aspirations of democracy. But does it ? Equality, we need to be
reminded, is not a fact, but an ideal—something
at which we have to aim. And one of the
main things we may hope for in a better
organised society is that the world will not lose
or waste so much of the intellectual genius in
its midst. We need all the eminence, intellectual, moral, artistic, that we can get—not
that the eminent individual may amass a
fortune or receive the fatal gift of the peerage
(as for those that care for such things—verily
they have their reward), but that he may exercise his gifts, as all the world's greatest men
would wish to exercise them, for the benefit of
his fellow-men. Mr. Galton seems indeed to
suggest that eminent men generally do come to
the front as it is ; but his statement is a little

[1] *Hereditary Genius*, p. 14.

rash, and he hardly counts the cost of the struggle.

"If the 'eminent' men of any period had been change-lings when babies, a very fair proportion [what does he consider such?] of those who survived and retained their health up to fifty years of age, would, notwithstanding their altered circumstances, have equally risen to eminence. Thus—to take a strong case—it is incredible that any combination of circumstances could have repressed Lord Brougham to the level of undistinguished mediocrity." (p. 38.)

Mr. Galton's example is well chosen for his purpose. Lord Brougham was just the kind of man who would anywhere have pushed himself into notoriety of some kind. But those social hindrances which "form a system of natural selection" may allow a great many Lord Broughams to come to the front in different disguises and yet may repress some who might do the world more service than an indefinite array of Lord Broughams. Supposing Mr. Darwin had had to pass his life as an over-worked and over-worried country surgeon or had been a factory hand in a huge manufactur-ing town, he might conceivably have been a noted man in a small naturalists' club and been laughed at by his neighbours for collecting

beetles; but would he have discovered the
origin of species and proved his discovery by
long years of continuous research? It is perfectly true that "social hindrances cannot im-
pede men of high ability from eminence," and
that "social advantages áre incompetent to give
that status to a man of moderate ability." But
"social hindrances" may exhaust all the energy
of the ablest in the bare struggle for existence,
and may direct the energy of those who do
succeed into wrong and mischievous channels.
We cannot invent a social machine for manu-
facturing genius, but we might do something
to eliminate the waste and misapplication of
genius that goes on at present. Commercial
competition and the fight for social pre-
eminence offer terrible temptations to the
scientific worker, the writer of books, the
artist.

Mr. Galton himself proposes what would
amount to a very considerable reorganisation
of society, and suggests some principles which
consistency and practical necessities might
oblige us to carry a little further :—

"The best form of civilisation in respect to the improvement of the race, would be one in which society was not

costly ; where incomes were chiefly derived from professional sources, and not much through inheritance; where
every lad had a chance of showing his abilities, and, if
highly gifted, was enabled to achieve a first-class education
and entrance into professional life, by the liberal help of
the exhibitions and scholarships which he had gained in
his early youth ; where marriage was held in as high honour
as in ancient Jewish times ; where the pride of race was
encouraged (of course I do not refer to the nonsensical
sentiment of the present day, that goes under that name);
where the weak could find a welcome and a refuge in
celibate monasteries or sisterhoods ; and lastly, where the
better sort of emigrants and refugees from other lands were
invited and welcomed, and their descendants naturalized."
(p. 362.)

On almost the last page of Mr. Galton's
book we have these words :—" The human
race can gradually modify its own nature."
(p. 375.) Take along with this a conclusion of
Darwin's :—" It may be doubted whether any
character can be named that is distinctive of a
race and is constant," [1] and I do not think there
remains much excuse for the conclusions of
fatalism and *laissez faire* that are often drawn
from the doctrine of heredity. Especially, if
we cannot trust to acquired habits being transmitted merely by descent, have we additional

---

[1] *Descent of Man*, p. 174.

reason for surrounding each successive generation of individuals, from their youth upwards,
with institutions and laws and customs that
will promote good and hinder bad tendencies.
The moral significance of the organisation of
society can hardly be over-estimated. It is
little use preaching kindliness and consideration for others and hoping that sympathetic
feelings will gradually become innate, if the
society into which individuals are born be
openly and confessedly a ceaseless struggle and
competition. For eighteen centuries a gospel
of peace and brotherhood has been preached
and *talked ;* but the child plays with a toy gun
and the youth sees the successful millionaire
held up as his model for imitation—the man
who boasts that he is " self-made," and who,
as the American remarked, has by that boast
" taken a great responsibility off the Almighty."
Not only education, but the very amusements
and healthy exercises of school life are all infected and corrupted by this diseased spirit of
competition. No wonder that those are scoffed
at or denounced who venture to think that a
society of rational beings might proceed more
rationally. From the fact that human societies,

like natural organisms, grow and are not made, we have certainly to learn that every evil cannot be remedied in a day. But from the other, at least equally important fact, that human societies do not merely grow but are consciously altered by human effort, we have also to learn that every evil is not to be accepted as inevitable. The spread of ideas regarding a better organisation of society is itself a factor in the attainment of that better organisation—not, of course, that we can make out a complete plan, like an architect, and then get it put into practice. Time and experience alone can suggest the details. But the teach- ing of evolutionary science, rightly understood, gives us no excuse for putting aside all schemes of social reorganisation as merely foolish and dreamy idealism. A fair study of social evolu- tion will at least indicate the direction in which we have to move.

§ 7. *THE LAW OF SOCIAL PROGRESS.*

Hitherto in my argument I have accepted the formulæ of " struggle for existence " and " natural selection " as quite sufficient to express the evolution of human society. They are quite accurate, if applied with a full recognition of the new elements which enter into the struggle over and above those operating in the biological sphere. But perhaps these formulæ, though accurate, hardly express the whole truth. Mr. Spencer's recognition of only two great types of society—the militant and the industrial—and his theory that social evolution ends in complete individualism are scarcely consistent with his own insistence on the organic or super-organic nature of society. Sir Henry Maine has only one great formula—that society advances from *status* to contract—and sticks there or else goes backwards. Is there not a higher type of society beyond and above each of these onesided extremes—cohesion without individual liberty and individual liberty of the negative sort without social cohesion?

In human society thought or reflection, as we have seen, enters in as a factor, lifting it above the merely natural organism, and so perhaps we may look at the nature of thought in order to find out the way in which society progresses. On every subject we think about we begin with some rough opinion, either received from others

·or the result of hasty observation. If we go on
to think about this opinion, we have to question
it, to examine it, and unless we come to a
standstill at the stage of doubt or criticism, we
go on to form some more adequate opinion,
which may indeed be only the old opinion in a
better form or may be something very different.
But this new opinion may in its turn be questioned in order to be corrected, and so on, for
the truth always proves itself more complex
than at first appeared : and, unless we lazily
acquiesce in dogmatic solutions, we cannot
cease from the labour of thinking. It might
indeed be more prudent to avoid mentioning
Hegel's name ; but this very commonplace pro-
·cess is his " dialectic method " in its simplest
and most familiar form. This "advance by
negation" is the way we have to think about
·everything. And if we apply this dialectic
method to society, what does it suggest ? That
we cannot rest in the critical or negative stage
·of modern individualism. But does that imply a
·return to the mediæval type of society ? to "the
good old days " of aristocratic and ecclesiastical
·domination ? By no means. It implies an
·advance to a stage in which all that is most

precious in individualism must be retained along
with the stability of social conditions which individualism has destroyed.   And this new stage
can be best described by the word " Socialism."

§ 8. *APPLICATIONS.*

By way of practical application, let us use
the light gained in our study of the nature of
social evolution generally to consider in detail
three great parts of the social problem : (1)
State interference with the condition of labour,
(2) the position of women, (3) the population
question, which is obviously connected with
both the preceding.

(1) Strauss, to whom I have referred before
as professedly applying the new faith of Evolution to the practical guidance of life, objects
even to trade-unions agitating for a reduction
of the hours of labour.[1]   He is so hot upon
the point that his patriotism, which elsewhere
seems to constitute the principal part of his
morality, deserts him here, and he suggests that

---

[1] *The Old Faith and the New*, sec. 83 in German edit.
1875 = sec. 79 (ii. p. 98) in Eng. Transl.

the employers of labour should "if necessary
send to foreign countries for workmen and then
let the refractory see who will be able to hold
out longest." This is the struggle à *outrance*,
though he makes no express reference to the
evolutionary formula here. Few thoughtful
Englishmen would now venture to go so far
as that and deliberately to propose, as Strauss
does, the complete suppression of the liberty of
association among the workmen, however much
they may envy autocratic methods and imitate
them, when they get the chance, on a small scale
and in a feeble way. But there are very many,
even of our most Radical politicians, who,
while allowing or encouraging trades-unions to
struggle for higher wages and a reduction of the
hours of labour, object to the State meddling at
all in the matter, except in the case of women
and children, or as J. S. Mill would have put
it, except in the case of children only. Adults
are to be left to shift for themselves. Well, we
know what that means. It is needless to use
any vivid or picturesque language. Those
who have eyes to see and ears to hear can see
and hear for themselves. This system of un-
checked competition—one cannot repeat it too

often—means a prodigal and frightful waste.
Some have to work too hard and too long:
others cannot get any work to do at all or get
it irregularly and uncertainly: others, who
might work, do not and will not—the idlers at
both ends of the social scale, the moral refuse
produced by our economic system. This
system is exactly what we find in nature
generally; but one would think that human
beings might use their reason to discover some
less wasteful scheme. Water will find its own
level; but how much mischief may it cause in
so doing?—mischief which can be avoided.
We have beautiful flowers or miserable weeds
in our gardens according as a skilful gardener
"interferes" or not; and when he thins out an
overcrowded bed, he need not throw away the
plants: there are many who would be glad
to have them. It is all one great problem of
distribution. Here is so much work needing to
be done and so many persons to do it. The
organisation of labour is not an easy task; but
is it hopeless? At least we might diminish the
*dis*organisation, which is the system of mere
nature, as that appears to rational beings.
Cannot human societies imitate the higher

forms of nature, not the lower, so as to contrive some scheme for the diminution of waste?

Strauss is afraid, because of the interests of civilisation. But the civilisation he thinks of is that of the antique type of society, a civilisation limited to the few—a cultured minority, consoling themselves for the loss of old religious beliefs by reading poetry and hearing concerts and operas, amid a subject-multitude treated with some consideration, like dependent and useful lower animals, but left to poverty and superstition. What can be worse for civilisation than that the more energetic and successful workers, managing to get constant employment, have, as at present, no sufficient leisure for the cultivation of their faculties? And when in the case of the greatest number all available energy is used up in the struggle to feed the body, what wonder that the soul is neglected—"where a soul can be discerned"? Leisure is necessary for culture : and a moderate amount of work is good for physical, mental and moral health— excess is bad for all three. Cannot leisure and work be better distributed, according to a rational instead of a hap-hazard system? In the attempt to substitute rational for non-

rational methods there is no denial of the
scientific truth of evolution, and there is an
application of the principle on which Strauss
himself insists so strongly, that "man must not
merely be an animal repeated, but must be
something more, something better."

(2) The claim of women to an equal share
with men in the advantages and responsibilities
of education and citizenship is very frequently
met by the objection that to grant this claim is
to fly in the face of nature. And the objection,
when it comes from the evolutionist, has a
certain plausibility. He points out, perhaps,
how advance in organic life goes along with increasing differentiation of sex—a rash assertion
n biology, but I have heard it made by a biologist. And so, it is asked, are not the advocates
of women's rights trying to reverse all that, and
to produce a morally asexual being ? Again,
if we limit ourselves to human society, it is
urged that "the difference between the sexes,
as regards the cranial cavity, increases with the
development of the race, so that the male
European excels much more the female, than
the negro the negress" (quoted from Vogt by
Darwin, *Descent of Man*, p. 566 *n.;* but it is

admitted that more observations are yet requisite before the fact can be positively asserted).
It is argued from this fact, *if such it be*, that the
progress of society has brought with it a still
greater differentiation of sex, and, this having
proved beneficial for the human race, it is folly
to seek to reverse it. Let us take the last
argument first. Because a certain method has
led us up to a certain point, it does not follow
that the same method continued will carry us
on further. Races that have reached a certain
stage may be hindered by extreme conservatism
from making any further progress—like the
Chinese. Again, at what degree of differentiation between the habits and lives of the sexes
are we to draw the line ? Englishmen, French-
men, Turks would draw it very differently.
And the Turk ought to please the biological
Conservative best, because he has pushed the
differentiation of the sexes to a logical issue.
The persons who use this kind of argument
fancy that they are influenced by scientific con-
siderations, but they are really influenced by
what they happen to have grown accustomed to.
Thirdly, *if* there is this greater difference
between the cranial cavities of savage and

civilised men than between those of savage and civilised women, to what must it be due?

(*a*) Those who believe that acquired characteristics (*i.e.* characteristics produced by agencies external to the organism) are transmitted, must explain this difference by the difference in institutions, laws and customs. Well, then—what these have done before in one direction they may do again in another. And the *same* education and the *same* responsibilities will, in course of time, put the average woman on the same level with the average man. (*b*) If use and disuse are not allowed as explanations, then this alleged brain inferiority of women must be due either to natural or to sexual selection. (*a*) If to *natural* selection, this would mean that in the struggle for existence those races or tribes have succeeded best in which the males have on the average had better brains than the females. And this *may* have been so in times when constant fighting was necessary for existence, though in such a case it would be the greater superiority of the male and not the greater relative inferiority of the female that had been the real cause of success. But this affords no argument that, when many other conditions of success than fighting power become necessary, the process of natural selection will continue to act in the same way. A people, *all* whose members become superior in mental qualities, will have the advantage over those peoples in which the development is partial and onesided; for, certainly, it could not be argued that the (alleged) relatively greater inferiority of the civilised female brain had gone along with an increased capacity for the purely physical functions of maternity, as compared with what is found among savage races. (*β*) If, on the other hand, the alleged difference is due to *sexual* selection, this must mean, not merely that men as a rule have preferred women with inferior brain power to their own (which is likely enough), but women whose female children were also on the average inferior in this respect to their male children. Supposing such a kind of selection to be possible (one can only admit it for the sake of argument), then, if men's ideas about women come to be altered, sexual selection will work in an opposite manner. With a new ideal of woman, the clever would be preferred to the stupid, and the

mother of clever daughters to the mother of
stupid daughters. Thus, *even if* the assertion
of Carl Vogt were true, it offers no conclusive
argument against the political and social equalisation of the sexes ; because this equalisation
would on *any* recognised principles of evolution,
bring about ultimately a natural equality. On
the whole, however, one may fairly retain the
suspicion that this alleged difference is not a
fact, and that the greater average eminence (in
the past) of men than of women in intellectual
pursuits is entirely due (as on any theory it
must be mostly due) to the effect of institutions
and customs and ideas operating within the
lifetime of the individual, and not to differences
physically inherited. Little girls are certainly
not on the average stupider than little boys :
and, if on the average men *show* more intellectual ability than women, may not this be
due to the way in which the two sexes are
respectively treated in the interval ?

But, even if there were an *average* mental
superiority in men due to sex-differentiation becoming greater with the attainment of maturity
(we have really no right to make definite asser-
tions on the subject, because women have never

yet had a fair chance of showing their capacities on a sufficiently large scale), Plato's argument would still hold that, though there may
be a general superiority of men, yet there are
many women superior to many men, and it is a
pity that the State should lose the advantage of
their services.[1]

With regard to the argument from nature
generally, even if we agree to the generalisation
that advance implies increasing differentiation
of sex and not the very reverse, it must be
insisted that *difference* is not the same thing
as *inequality* (though the two are very apt to
be confounded), and that the very difference
between the sexes is a reason why the State
should not disregard the opinions and the feelings of half, or in old countries more than half,
the population.

But the main point is really this : that society
has enabled man to rise above the mere animal
and, as has been pointed out, to be influenced
not merely by natural pressure but by *ideas*.
The idea of equality has grown up—I shall not
at present inquire how far it is due to the universal citizenship of the Roman Empire and to

[1] *Republic,* v. 455.

the widening conceptions of Roman Law, how
far to the Stoic philosophy with its brotherhood
of mankind, and how far to Christianity as an
inter-national or non-national religion, declaring
the equality of all before God, though carrying
with it the Judaic supremacy of the male sex.
When this idea of equality was proclaimed in
the American revolution, the negro slaves were
conveniently overlooked; when it was proclaimed
in the French revolution, the existence of a
whole sex seemed to be forgotten by every
one but Condorcet.   And there are many old-
fashioned Radicals still, who lack sufficient faith
in their own creed to apply it in a thorough-
going way.   How often does one hear the argument, " Oh, but women are naturally Conservative, and if they had political power, we
should be governed by the priests."   It may
rather be said that the instability of republican
government in France has been very much due
to its not having appealed to the sympathies of
the mothers of the French people.   If women
are expressly and purposely kept in the patriarchal stage of social evolution, is it wonderful
that their feelings and sympathies mostly
correspond to an antique social type ?   It is

hypocritical to deny the political capacity of
women, simply because their political *in*capacity
has through long centuries been diligently cultivated ; but this is always the favourite sort of
argument with the jealous champions of privilege :—first to prevent a race or class or sex
from acquiring a capacity, and then to justify
the refusal of rights on the grounds of this
absence—to shut up a bird in a narrow cage and
then pretend to argue with it that it is incapable
of flying. What is the reason of the power
which the Catholic Church possesses over the
minds of women, except that the Church alone
offers them any escape into a larger circle of
interests than those of the patriarchal family ?
They do not reflect that the Church brands
them with a stamp of inferiority,[1] that did not

[1] Even the cult of the Madonna, which is a revival of the
female element in deity, did not do away with the degrada-
tion of the woman. There is a story (given in Grimm's
Household Tales, Note to Tale 139) of St. Bernard, that he
once went into a Cathedral to pay his devotions to the
image of the Virgin. He fell twice on his knees before it,
and full of fervour uttered the words, " Oh, gracious, mild,
and highly favoured mother of God." Hereupon the image
began to speak, and said, " Welcome, my Bernard ! " But
the saint, who was displeased by this, reprimanded the
Queen of Heaven for speaking, in these words, "Silence !

exist in the old Aryan religions, which had their
gods and goddesses, priests and priestesses.
They do feel that the rule of the priest may be
something higher than the rule of the household despot. Religious teachers have understood that their success must depend on their
winning the mothers of the race. When will
political leaders come to recognise the same ?

No woman is to speak in the congregation !" This is an
admirable illustration of the ecclesiastical and sentimental
theory of womanhood—a worship that professes to exalt
woman—whether the Madonna or *das Ewig-Weibliche*—
above man, combined with a refusal of rationality that sinks
her beneath him. The same thing appears in quarters
where we should less expect it. Thus we find the late Mr.
Laurence Oliphant, who with many protests against the cor-
ruption of the Churches, builds up on a strangely unscientific foundation what professes to be a new "scientific"
religion, and who proclaims a higher code of morals, based
mainly on the elevation of women, yet denouncing, like a
Catholic or a Comtist priest, the agitation for "women's
rights" and "the higher education of women," and maintaining the very retrograde and (in these days) immoral
doctrine that women have *no responsibility* with regard to
public affairs. (*Scientific Religion*, pp. 316, 324.) In fact, the
"Divine Feminine" or "Woman"—with a very big capital—
is one of the worse enemies that women have to contend
with in their struggle towards recognition as complete and
responsible human *persons*.

Mr. Herbert Spencer [1] is afraid that women, if admitted now to political life, might do mischief by introducing the ethics of the family into the State. " Under the ethics of the family the greatest benefits must be given where the merits are smallest, under the ethics of the State the benefits must be proportioned to the merits." Mr. Spencer seems to have more confidence than most of us would in applying the strict principle of geometrical proportion to distributive justice. Do people get benefits in proportion to their merits in any society we have ever seen or are likely to see? *And would those persons whose merits are greatest care most for the greatest rewards?* Is it right to separate the ethics of the family, in Mr. Spencer's favourite antithetic fashion, from the ethics of the State? If something is right in a family, it is difficult to see why it is *therefore*, without any further reason, wrong in the State. If the participation of women in politics means that, as a good family educates all its members, so must a good State, what better issue could there be? The family ideal of the State may be difficult of attainment, but, as an ideal, it is

[1] *Sociology*, pp. 793, 794.

better than the policeman theory.[1]   It would
mean the moralisation of politics.   The cultiva-

[1] In the same notice in *Mind* to which I have referred,.
above (page 41, *note*) the writer says this passage is inconsistent with page 68, where I speak of the patriarchal stage
of social evolution as already transcended.   Does he really
suppose the ethics of the family, in Mr. Spencer's sense,
to belong to the patriarchal stage of society?   By the patriarchal stage I understand what Maine and all other writers
on the subject mean by it—the stage which is prior to
political society in the proper sense.   On page 68 I argue
that to refuse to women the duties and responsibilities of
full citizenship is injurious to the common weal, because half
the adult population is thus kept (so far as institutions can
keep them) in the mental and moral condition of "survivals"
from a superseded stage of society.   Here I am arguing that
Mr. Spencer is mistaken in making an absolute antithesis
between the ethics of the family and the ethics of the State.
What is right in the smaller association cannot, I contend,.
be *ultimately* wrong in the larger, though it may be more
difficult of attainment.   I should indeed wish to amend Mr.
Spencer's formula for the ethics of the family ("greatest
benefits where the merits are smallest "), first of all by giving
up the fallacious appearance of mathematical exactness and,
secondly, by ceasing to talk about " merits."   A baby may
receive the greatest amount of care in a household, but not
because its merits are smallest.   I should prefer to say:
" Every one to work according to capacity : every one to
receive according to need, so far as compatible with the
well-being of the family as a whole."   (Of course "capacity"
and " need " are not the same things as " wishes.")   Is not
this our *ideal* of family ethics?   And, if it is a right ideal,.

tion of separate sorts of virtues and separate ideals of duty in men and women has led to the whole social fabric being weaker and un-healthier than it need be.

The history of the position of women is much more complex than is often represented. It is not true to say that the *status* of women has *always* improved in direct ratio to the general advance. The patriarchal stage repre-sents on the whole a higher type of civilisation than the matriarchal. But, it is to be observed, those societies which have exaggerated the patriarchal type and built all their civilisation upon it, seem to be incapable of advancing further. This is conspicuously the case with Mohammedan peoples. Just as war has ful-filled important functions in the progress of the human race, so the terrible powers of the house-father in certain ancient systems of law have had their use : but it does not follow that what once aided the race in its struggle with

must it not come to be our ideal of social ethics generally, because it is the system which would involve the least waste of life and energy ? Of course the compromise of equality is frequently needed to save disputes, and so avoid waste in another way.

other races will continue to do so when the struggle becomes of a higher and more complex kind.[1]

The objection is sometimes made that, in countries where it is considered necessary to have compulsory military service for all males, it would be unjust and inexpedient that women should have a voice in political matters. This objection would be easily met by compelling all women physically fit for it to undergo training as nurses, and making them liable to be called upon to serve as such in time of war.[2] And this training would be more useful to them and,

---

[1] "Such is the nature of men that, when they have reached their ends by a certain road, they cannot understand that, the times being different, success may be won by other methods and the old ways are no longer of use." These words represent the theme of the 9th chap. of Machiavelli's *Discourses on Livy*, Bk. iii.

[2] A probably reverend reviewer in the *Guardian* has understood this passage, as if I imagined an army of "four-and-twenty fighting men and five-and-twenty"—nurses ! In the very next sentence I suggest that nurses are useful elsewhere than in military hospitals. I quite admit, however, that until all service for the community, whether it be fighting the enemy in the field or fighting disease in the sick-room, come to be treated as "public service," we can have no genuine social equality. This is implied in the next paragraph.

to the whole community in time of peace than his military training is to the peasant or artisan.

Of all the objections made to the equality of the sexes the only one that deserves very serious attention is that made by Sir James Fitzjames Stephen in his clever attack on J. S. Mill. He points out (in *Liberty, Equality, Fraternity,*[1]) that women may suffer more than they have done, if plunged into a nominally equal but really unequal contest in the already overcrowded labour market. The conclusion usually drawn from this argument is a sentimental reaction in favour of the old family ideal (for instance in Mr. Besant's books). There is another alternative, and that is the socialistic. The elevation of the *status* of women and the regulation of the conditions of labour are *ultimately* inseparable questions. On the basis of individualism I cannot see how it is possible to answer the objections of Sir J. Fitzjames Stephen.

---

[1] Pp. 253, 254. (Edit. 2.) Sir J. F. Stephen sees quite clearly what is hid from the eyes of many Liberals, that the change from status to contract produces "not equality but inequality in its harshest and least sympathetic form" (p. 249).

(3) I began by referring to Malthus, and
with Malthus I must end.   Socialists have
usually brushed aside the Malthusian precepts
and somewhat too lightly neglected the Malthusian arguments.   To some extent this has
been due to a correct instinct.   The "pru-
dence" of the old school of political economy
would mean that the most careful and intelligent part of the population should leave the
continuance of the race mainly to the least
careful and the least intelligent portion—thus
bringing about a survival of the unfittest.   And
so the theory of natural selection, which was
suggested to Darwin by Malthus's theory of
population, has come to be used as a refutation
of Malthus's practical suggestions.[1]   Socialist
views on the question have not always had so
scientific a basis, but have sometimes rested on
nothing much better than the popular superstition that where God sends mouths he sends
the food to feed them, though this may be dis-
guised in a non-theological form, such as "the
earth is capable of producing abundance of
food for all its inhabitants."   Now what does
this mean ?   That the earth at present may be

[1] Cp. Galton's *Hereditary Genius*, p. 356.

made to bear more than it now does, and that therefore it will maintain more than its present number of inhabitants, is true enough. But only a complete failure to grasp the meaning of the struggle for existence, and the relation between increase of means of subsistence and increase of population could lead any one to maintain that, absolutely, the earth can be made capable of supporting an indefinitely increasing number of inhabitants. If the checks on population supplied by famine, war, pestilence and vice be removed in any large measure, the increase would in time outrun any possible increase in the means of subsistence, even with all that improved appliances and diminished waste could do. Here, as elsewhere, human beings must raise themselves above unthinking animals and not trust to a kind Providence in which they take no part. The course of events, if left to itself, will act in the way that we do, when we dispose of superfluous puppies and kittens, but not quite so rapidly and mercifully. We must become provident for ourselves. But what is to be said of the Darwinian objection, the protest " against the higher races being encouraged to withdraw from the struggle for existence"? That would be a valid objection, if we suppose the present system of free competition in the labour market to continue for ever. If employers of labour remain a separate class (instead of becoming directors of labour, acting solely on behalf of the whole community), and are free to import the labour of cheaper and more prolific races, as we have seen even the patriotic Strauss suggesting, there would certainly be a continuous degeneration of the species. But, most assuredly, the day will come and very soon, when the workers of all the more civilised nations will join together not to undersell each other; and by that time employers will not be absolutely free to import Chinese or Malays, who would practically be slaves of a new type.

It might, however, be objected that if the more civilised nations keep their numbers fairly on a level with the means of subsistence at home, there will no longer be the stream of emigrants pouring forth from our shores to civilise the world and develop the resources of new countries: "the abler races" will be "withdrawing from the struggle for existence." There are some people who seem to think that

an unlimited supply of what we call the Anglo-
Saxon race is the best remedy for all the evils
of the world. Well, without wishing to be
needlessly unpatriotic, I do not think the unlimited Anglo-Saxon is an altogether unmitigated blessing. The filibuster, the mercantile
adventurer and the missionary have not been
so perfectly successful between them in dealing
with the problem of the lower races ; for the
mere disappearance of lower races before the
rum supplied by the trader and the clothes en-
joined by the missionary (to the great profit of
the Lancashire manufacturer) is not quite a
satisfactory solution. What has been already
said about the transmission of a type of culture,
irrespective of the continuity of the race that
first developed it, seems to help one here. We
need have less doubt of the excellence of our
language and of our literature and of some of
our institutions than of the supreme excellence
of our race : and there is nothing to prevent
distant tribes and nations regarding Europe,
and Britain not least, as the school or university
to which they shall send their most promising
youth in order to adopt just as much of our
civilisation as suits them, so that they may

work out their problems in their own manner. That would surely be a healthier way in which the higher might affect the lower races · in the future, educating them instead of enslaving, demoralising or destroying them.

As to the adjustment of population to subsistence, Mr. H. Spencer has sufficient faith in the beneficence of nature to believe this will come about of itself through a biological law—that multiplication and individuation vary inversely, so that, as the physical and intellectual culture of the individual is more and more attended to, the increase of the species will gradually diminish. This "law" is, however, as yet only a mere speculation of Mr. Spencer's. There does seem to be in the world a certain amount of what we may call natural adaptation, which leads the more cultured and the more settled nations to be less prolific than those of the same race or stock who are living in new countries with plenty of elbow-room. The English race in Western America or in Australia does seem to be more fruitful than in old England or in New England. But the whole theory is a very doubtful one. And a rational adaptation of means to ends seems requisite to obtain the desired result. This is pre-eminently a question which can only receive proper consideration and solution when women are admitted to full social and political responsibility. It is the woman who bears the suffering of maternity and has the care of the very young, and so the woman is more immediately interested than the man. So long as women were brought up to believe that their sole or main function in life was to bear children, and were made to feel that there was something not only of disadvantage but of disgrace in being unmarried or childless, what wonder that population has been increased indefinitely and recklessly? Every inducement was in that direction, the ideas of a military society, the influence of the clergy (and, at least in Protestant countries, their example also), the employment of child-labour before the factory acts, the system of our old poor law —everything encouraged the natural tendency of the race to increase. With a change in the prevalent sentiment, a change in fact will certainly follow. When women have other interests in the world than those of maternity, things will not go on so blindly as before. And the race need not necessarily suffer thereby, but

the very reverse.   Fewer children will be born,
but fewer will die, fewer will be sickly.   Those
who are born will be better and more intelli-
gently cared for.   Two healthy, well reared
children will be more useful to the community
than a dozen neglected waifs and strays.   Here,
again, we shall only be imitating by rational
procedure the upward tendency of nature,
which consists in the economy of production.
Rational selection will take the place of the
cruel process of natural selection.

If we are still reminded that only through
struggle can mankind attain any good thing, let
us remember that there is a struggle from
which we can never altogether escape—the
struggle *against* nature, including the blind
forces of human passion.   There will always
be enough to do in this ceaseless struggle to
call forth all the energies of which human
nature at its very best is capable.   At present,
how much of these energies, intellectual and
moral as well as physical, is wasted in mutual
destruction !   May we not hope that by degrees
this mutual conflict will be turned into mutual
help ?   And, if it is pointed out that even at
present mutual help does come about, even

through mutual conflict, indirectly and with much loss on the way, may we not hope to make that mutual help conscious, rational, systematic, and so to eliminate more and more the suffering going on around us ?

II.

NATURAL SELECTION AND THE SPIRITUAL WORLD.

"DARWINISM," the title of the delightful book which Mr. Alfred Russel Wallace published in 1889, is a splendid proof of an absence of jealousy not too common, even in scientific minds ; but it is also an express declaration of what Mr. Wallace understands by the evolution theory. Mr. Wallace is more "Darwinian" than Darwin himself. Darwin put forward "natural selection" as only one among the factors of organic evolution : he did not attempt to set aside the old Lamarckian theory of the hereditary transmission of the effects of use and disuse, although natural selection was his own discovery—a discovery made independently by himself and by Mr. Wallace. It has been lately said by Professor Patrick Geddes,[1] that there is at the present time "a growing tendency to limit the impor-

[1] *Evolution of Sex*, p. 304.

tance of natural selection." This statement will
doubtless cause great satisfaction to the Duke
of Argyll; but I do not know what proof can
be given for its truth, except the opinion of
Professor Geddes himself, of Mr. Herbert
Spencer, and of a few American biologists;
according to biologists such as Mr. Russel
Wallace, Professor Weismann, and Mr. E. B.
Poulton, the tendency is now all the other way.
And this is admitted by Mr. Grant Allen (in
spite of his admiration for Spencerian psychology) in a very remarkable review of Professor
Weismann's papers *On Heredity*, in the
Academy of February 1, 1890. In any case,
there is this difference between natural selection and the other alleged factors of organic
evolution, that they are speculations, more or
less metaphysical in character, whereas natural
selection is a fact; it is a cause actually at
work in nature, and the only question is,
whether it is able or not to explain all the
phenomena. On the other hand, Mr. Spencer's
" differentiation and integration," Professor
Geddes's see-saw of "anabolism and katabo-
lism," Mr. Cope's " bathmism" or growth-force,
which acts by means of retardation and acceler-

ation (and which Mr. Darwin found himself quite unable to understand), remind us of the theories about Nature that were thrown out by the older Greek philosophers—above all, of the " love and strife " in the poetic system of Empedocles. Such general formulæ may help to make the universe more intelligible to us, and may possibly suggest profitable lines of investigation to the inquirer, who is otherwise too bewildered by details ; but they stand on a perfectly different level from the everywhere present fact of the struggle for existence, in which those organisms that happen to possess useful variations have a better chance of succeeding and transmitting these useful qualities to offspring than those less favourably equipped. The hereditary transmission of the effects of use and disuse has been very readily accepted by the popular imagination, and has indeed bulked most largely in current versions of evolution, because it has fitted in perfectly well with traditional beliefs about hereditary curses, and with the theological doctrine of " original sin." " The fathers have eaten sour grapes, and the children's teeth are set on edge." People who make stale jokes about the ancestral ape wearing off his tail by sedentary habits imagine that they are putting *Darwin's* theory in a comic light, but have probably never taken the trouble to understand natural selection.[1] The facts which, it has been supposed, can only be explained by the transmission of the effects of use and disuse, turn out, however, either not to be facts at all—a misfortune that often happens to " facts "—or to admit of a perfectly satisfactory explanation by the *cessation* of natural selection. Thus the various contrivances of civilisation, including spectacles, make defective vision less injurious to human beings

[1] Here are two stanzas of a song on " The Origin of Species " by a late learned and witty Scotch judge. They are entirely " Lamarckian," though probably intended, and certainly generally believed, to represent Darwin's theory.

" A deer with a neck that was longer by half
　Than the rest of its family's (try not to laugh),
　By stretching and stretching became a giraffe,
　　Which nobody can deny."

　　　*　　　*　　　*　　　*　　.　*

" The four-footed beast that we now call a whale
　Held his hind-legs so close that they grew to a tail,
　Which it uses for threshing the sea like a flail,
　　Which nobody can deny."

Songs and Verses by " An Old Contributor to Maga." p. 3.

now-a-days than it was in the hunting stage;
and thus the prevalence of shortsightedness, so
far as it cannot be accounted for by what takes
place in the individual life-time, does not com-
pel us to suppose that it has been produced by
the hard study of past generations "poring
over miserable books." At least the cautious
verdict with regard to the transmission of the
effects of use and disuse appears to be " not
proven."

Mr. Wallace even rejects Darwin's theory of
sexual selection, except in so far as it consists
merely in the struggle between males and can
therefore be resolved into one aspect of natural
selection.[1] So that no one could apply the
theory of natural selection in a more complete
and thorough-going way than Mr. Wallace—
until he comes to the middle of his very last
chapter. He fully accepts " Mr. Darwin's conclusion as to the essential identity of man's
bodily structure with that of the higher
mammalia, and his descent from some ancestral form common to man and the anthropoid
apes"; but, when Darwin goes on to derive
the moral nature and mental faculties of man

[1] *Darwinism*, pp. 274, 283, 296.

from their rudiments in the lower animals in the same manner and by the action of the same general laws as his physical structure, Mr. Wallace refuses to follow him. He holds that there is a " spiritual world," and that just as the glacial epoch supervened on the geologic causes previously in operation, so an " influx" from this spiritual world has produced man's moral sense, his mathematical, artistic and metaphysical faculties.[1] He considers himself driven to this supposition because he believes that these faculties cannot be accounted for by natural selection. Yet, after saying this, Mr. Wallace declares at the very end of his book that " the Darwinian theory, even when carried out to its extreme logical conclusion, not only does not oppose, but lends a decided support to a belief in the spiritual nature of man. It shows us how man's body may have been developed from that of a lower animal form under the law of natural selection ; but it also teaches us that we possess intellectual and moral faculties which could not have been so developed, but must have had another origin ; and for this origin we can only find an adequate cause in

[1] *Ibid.* p. 463 ; comp. p. 476.

the unseen universe of Spirit."[1]   Now, however
true Mr. Wallace's beliefs about the spiritual
world may be, it does seem odd to say that
they are a carrying out of the Darwinian theory
" to its extreme logical conclusion." One has
heard of the young officer who said that Alder-
shot was a very nice place—to get away from,
and of the schoolboy (was he Irish ?) who de-
fined sugar as " what makes your tea so nasty
when you don't put any in "; and so we may
say that the Darwinian theory supports Mr.
Wallace's views, when he gets away from it,
and when it is *not* applied to mental and moral
evolution. This " spiritual world," which is
postulated in order to account for the moral
sense and the higher mathematics, is also to
serve as an explanation of " the marvellously
complex forces which we know as gravitation,
cohesion, chemical force, radiant force and
electricity, without which the material universe
could not exist for a moment in its present form,
and perhaps not at all, since without these
forces, and perhaps others which may be termed
atomic, it is doubtful whether matter itself could
have any existence.   And still more surely can

[1] *Ibid.* p. 478.

we refer to it those progressive manifestations
of Life in the vegetable, the animal and man—
which we may classify as unconscious, conscious
and intellectual life—and which probably depend upon different degrees of spiritual influx."[1]
Now, if gravitation, cohesion, etc., are the
spiritual world, the ordinary man may well ask,
"Where is the non-spiritual world?" and an
idealist philosopher, where such can be found,
will echo the question in a slightly different
tone. Nobody denies that gravitation, chemical affinity, life, consciousness, intelligence, represent an ascending scale. But if the word
"spiritual" be extended to the lowest of them,
does this mean anything very different from
extending the word "material" to the highest
of them ? There is, indeed, a difference between naming the ultimate principle of the universe from the higher end of the scale or from
the lower ; but it is a difference in ontological
theory and not on a question of physical causation, with which alone the biologist, as such,
has to deal.

Leaving this matter for the present, let us
see what reasons Mr. Wallace has for rejecting

[1] *Ibid.* p. 476.

natural selection as an explanation of the moral and intellectual nature of man. At first sight one is rather startled by the fact that, in order to prove that these are not derived from the rudiments of them in the lower animals, Mr. Wallace takes, not some characteristic that seems to belong to all men and no animals—a characteristic such as Professor Max Müller considers language to be—Mr. Wallace takes the mathematical, musical and artistic faculties, which, as he himself insists, are to be found only in a very small number of human beings. According to the somewhat arbitrary statistics of the schoolmasters consulted by Mr. Wallace, only about 1 per cent. of the boys in an English public school "have any special taste or capacity for mathematical studies," and only about 1 per cent., again, "have real or decided musical talent."[1]   The line of argument appears to be as follows : (1) These faculties, not being useful to man in the struggle for existence, could not have been developed by natural selection. (2) If they had been so developed, they would have been present among human beings with some approach to equality.

[1] *Ibid.* pp. 470, 471.

§ 2. *THE EVOLUTION OF MORALITY.*

The question of the origin of the moral sense is put aside in *Darwinism*[1] as " far too vast and complex to be discussed " there; but some discussion of it cannot well be avoided, because it forms the best initial test of the adequacy or inadequacy of the theory of natural selection outside the merely biological domain. The late Professor Clifford's brilliant, but too brief, contribution to ethics contains a more thorough-going application of the theory of natural selection to moral ideas than is to be found even in Darwin's *Descent of Man;* for Darwin, in rather hesitating fashion, was still inclined to admit the transmission of acquired habits.[2] Natural selection is also the principle of explanation adopted in Mr. Leslie Stephen's *Science of Ethics*, and, more explicitly still, in Mr. S. Alexander's *Moral Order and Progress.*

To put the matter very briefly : Man starts with social instincts of the same kind as are to be found developed in different degrees among

[1] p. 462.

[2] *E.g.*, p. 125 (edit. 2). " We may expect that virtuous habits will grow stronger, becoming perhaps fixed by inheritance."

the lower animals—and when we say " instincts"
it is as well to remember what Mr. Wallace
himself has so emphatically pointed out with
regard to the lower animals : " Much of the
mystery of instinct arises from the persistent
refusal to recognise the agency of imitation,
memory, observation and reason as often forming part of it." [1] The social instincts of man
cause him to live in groups ; and the struggle
for existence is carried on, not merely between
individual and individual, but between group
and group, this second type of struggle leading
to a mitigation of the fierceness of the struggle
within any particular group. Thus, it is to the
advantage of a tribe to have as many capable
fighting members as possible : they are no
longer mere rivals for food, but comrades in
pursuit of a common end. Those qualities that
tend to the success of the tribe in its contests
with other tribes are " selected " for survival,
because the tribes that display opposite qualities fail and are destroyed. What promotes the
welfare of the tribe is approved ; what hinders
it is condemned. " Conscience," as Clifford
puts it, " is the tribal self." We must not, and

[1] *Darwinism,* p. 442.

need not, suppose any deliberate reflection in a primitive stage. In conduct, as in other regions of Nature, variations take place "spontaneously"—*i.e.*, they happen to take place—how, or why, they take place is, as yet, a matter of pure speculation. The favourable variations are selected—*i.e.*, the unfavourable variations lead to the failure and extinction of the organisms which display them. It is the same principle of natural selection which applies to variations in structure and functions, in habits, in implements : useful variations are continually being "selected," prior to any deliberate reflection about the adaptation of means to ends. Thus, in the ethical sphere, we have a selection of types of conduct ; and these, the product of natural struggle and not of reflection, are the earliest moral ideals. Now all this has been put, as clearly as possible, by Mr. Wallace himself, in his earlier work, *Contributions to the Theory of Natural Selection* (1870), pp. 312, 313 :—

"Capacity for acting in concert for protection and for the acquisition of food and shelter ; sympathy, which leads all in turn to assist each other ; the sense of right, which checks depredations upon our fellows ; the smaller development of the combative and destructive propensities ; self-restraint in present appetites ; and that intelligent foresight which pre-

pares for the future, are all qualities, that from their earliest
appearance, must have been for the benefit of each community, and would, therefore, have become the subjects for
natural selection. . . . Tribes in which such mental
or moral qualities were predominant would, therefore, have
an advantage in the struggle for existence over other tribes
in which they were less developed, would live and maintain
their numbers, while the others would decrease and finally
succumb."

But for the evolution of morality it is not
necessary that the struggle should always go
so far as the extinction of all the individuals
practising a hurtful custom. Successful types
of custom are *imitated*, and the disappearance
of injurious customs before their successful rival
customs may take the place of the disappearance
of the persons or tribes who practise the injurious customs. It is a further step, and a
step that, more than anything else, marks the
rise of civilisation out of barbarism, when deliberate *reflection* leads a group of human beings
to change their customs in order to escape the
penalties of suffering and extinction which come
from a blind adherence to old customs that once
promoted the well-being of the community, but
in changed circumstances have now become
hurtful. Natural selection does not cease to
operate; but the conflict of ideas takes the

place of the competition of animal organisms. *Imitation* and *reflection* impose a check ont he mere physical struggle for existence ; but, according to this evolutionist theory of morality, they are themselves the product of natural selection, and not of a distinct cause ; and in the effects which they produce upon customs and ideas, the principle of natural selection is not left behind, but applied in a new sphere.

The growth of morality implies, of course, an advance in brain development, by the elimination within each group of the inferior members, and, in the struggle between groups, of the inferior groups. Further, we must notice the immense acceleration of progress rendered possible by language ; and Mr. Wallace does not seem to deny that the most complex of human languages differs only in degree from the sounds and gestures by which animals convey their feelings and emotions to one another. Language renders possible the transmission of experience irrespective of transmission by heredity. By means of language and of social institutions we inherit the acquired experience, not of our ancestors only, but of other races in the same sense of " inheritance " in which we talk of people inheriting land or furniture or railway shares. Language renders possible an accumulation of experience, a storing up of achievements, which makes advance rapid and secure among human beings in a way impossible among the lower animals. Indeed, might we not define civilisation in general as the sum of those contrivances which enable human beings to advance independently of heredity? Civilisation is healthiest when it works along with heredity. Mankind never becomes completely independent of the effects of heredity. And the highest civilisation falling to the inheritance of a decaying race will not prevent, and may even hasten its decay and extinction. On the other hand, though the race perishes, the civilisation need not be lost, but may be handed on to worthier and more capable heirs.

Consciousness, reflection, language, are all obviously advantages in the struggle for existence to the beings possessing them ; and it is much the simplest hypothesis to ascribe the origin of all of them to natural selection, instead of postulating a mysterious intrusion from without. As Mr. Wallace himself says :

"In a scientific inquiry a point which can be proved should not be assumed, and a totally unknown power should not be brought in to explain facts when known powers may be sufficient."[1]   But once there, consciousness, reflection, language, carry human beings rapidly a long way from the point at which those animals were, among whom these variations first appeared.   Mr. Wallace contends that the large brains of savages and the absence of hair from the greater part of the surface of the body are both inexplicable on the theory of natural selection.[2]   Big brains and bare backs are, he thinks, no advantage to the savage, and therefore cannot be the subjects of natural selection. Is that so?   The hairless *homo* with only a gorilla's brain would obviously be at a disadvantage compared with the gorilla, and would therefore disappear; but the disadvantage of a hairless skin has been more than compensated by the greater size of the brain. The hairy covering has ceased to be a necessity, and therefore has not been selected; and natural selection has thus offered no impedi-

[1] *Contributions to the Theory of Natural Selection*, p. 205.
[2] *Ibid.* p. 348.

ment to the probable operation of sexual selection (in Darwin's sense) in furthering its disappearance. Greater brain development has
allowed the luxury of sexual selection to
operate without fatal results to the race. In
any case, the greater the brain power, the less
the necessity of a hairy covering. Nay, the
progress of a hairless race has been brought
about by the very needs of clothing and shelter
adapted to varying circumstances, but only
where these needs could be met because of
greater brain development. Thus the difficulties raised by Mr. Wallace with regard to
these two differences between man and the
animals taken separately, disappear when they
are taken together.

Mr. Wallace himself[1] argues that the power
possessed by savages of travelling through
trackless forests comes not from instinct but
from the use of the perceptive and reasoning
faculties. Does not that imply the require-
ment of very considerable brain power ? The
civilised man uses his slightly greater brain
power in many different ways, and therefore
fails where the savage succeeds, his observa-

[1] *Contributions to the Theory of Natural Selection*, p. 207.

tion and his memory of what he has perceived
being much less exact.   As to the fact that the
hair has disappeared from the back of *homo*,
but not completely from the chest, is not that
correlated with the adoption of the erect position ? and that, again, with the differentiation
of hands and feet ?   And the advantage in
both these differences between man and the
lower animals is to be found in the use of
missiles and tools.

Mr. Wallace, in his treatment of the moral
sense, raises the usual Intuitionist objections to
Utilitarianism.   He holds that "there is a
feeling, a sense of right and wrong in our
nature, antecedent to and independent of experiences of utility."[1]   Now, it is just the
application of the theory of natural selection
in ethics that has removed the force of the
Intuitionist objections to the pre-evolutionist
Utilitarianism.   It was easy enough to point
out that men's moral judgments are not as a
rule based on calculations of consequences,
but are the result of unreflecting feeling.
To the Evolutionist ethics this is no objection.   The theory of natural selection makes

[1] *Contributions to the Theory of Natural Selection*, p. 354.

it a necessity that those societies should survive in which the promptings of the tribal self have been most felt ; and the mysterious " feelings " on which the Intuitionist falls back are thus accounted for. At the same time it is perfectly easy for the Evolutionist to explain why some virtues have been earlier recognised than others, and why the same acts have in different times and places been regarded as good or bad—standing difficulties to the Intuitionist. When reflection appears, however, a higher form of morality becomes possible ; the useful—*i.e.*, what conduces to the welfare of the social organism, is not recognised merely by the failure of those societies in which it is not pursued, but by deliberate reflection on the part of the more thoughtful members of the society. The utilitarian reformer reflects for his society, and anticipates and obviates the cruel process of natural selection by the more peaceful methods of legislative change. The theory of natural selection thus gives a new meaning to Utilitarianism. The beginnings of morality are explained, and Utilitarianism is thus saved from the reproach of being applicable only to highly developed races. And, secondly, the well-being of society, as the ethical end, is substituted for the individualist conception of a balance of pleasures and pains. " Happiness," says Professor Clifford, " is not the end of right action. My happiness is of no use to the community, except in so far as it makes me a more efficient citizen ; that is to say, it is rightly desired as a means and not as an end."[1]

Natural selection can be likewise applied to the explanation of the origin and development of social and political institutions, provided that sufficient account be taken of imitation and reflection, as produced by natural selection and yet counteracting the merely animal struggle for existence ; provided also it be recognised that an idea or institution may supplant another without the individuals concerned being necessarily killed off in the process. Natural selection operates in the highest types of human society as well as in the rest of the organic realm ; but it passes into a higher form of itself, in which the conflict of ideas and institutions takes the place of the struggle for existence between individuals and races.

[1] *Lectures and Essays*, ii. p. 173.

§ 3. *INTELLECTUAL EVOLUTION.*

The mathematical, the musical and the artistic faculties, the metaphysical faculty and "the peculiar faculty of wit and humour" are considered by Mr. Wallace to supply the strongest arguments for the insufficiency of natural selection to account for mental evolution. They are, he argues, of no use to savages, and yet men must have these faculties latent in them, because they appear, though in very different degrees, among civilised races. Now, in the first place, is it true that the mathematical faculty and the musical faculty are of no use to the lower races in their struggle for existence? Undoubtedly, the primitive savage who became abstracted over a mathematical problem, like Archimedes, would die of starvation, if he did not rather help to ward off the same calamity from wild beasts or other wild men ; but the savage who could count more than five would have an advantage over his rivals who never got beyond the fingers of one hand ; the mother who could not count her children would succeed in rearing fewer than the mother whose domestic arithmetic was always accurate ; and the people who believed that two and two made five, whether on this planet or on that other feigned by John Stuart Mill, would be at a disadvantage in fighting with the people who had established the doctrine that two and two made four. Plato says that Agamemnon would have been a poor sort of general if he had not been able to count his own feet ; and Mr. Wallace himself admits the military advantage possessed by the Romans in their engineering skill. An Archimedes, though perhaps less useful as a heavy-armed soldier than a stupider man, was certainly of service to his fellow-citizens in the carrying on of war.

Elementary arithmetic and elementary perceptions of spatial relations would undoubtedly be useful to men living even under the rudest conditions, and the brains capable of very simple mathematical thinking may well enough be the ancestors of brains capable of more complex processes, if the capacity has been accumulated by favourable combinations of parents occurring again and again. It is not difficult to account for the fact that mathematical genius of a high order is sporadic, and

rare even amongst the most civilised peoples.
Mathematical genius of a high order, not being
useful to the individual or the tribe under rude
conditions, nor even under more advanced conditions, has not been selected as a characteristic
of the species *homo* (in the way in which the
capacity for language has been) ; nor has it
become the special characteristic of any marked
division of mankind, like any particular race-
characteristic. Under rude conditions such
high scientific capacity would even be injurious ; under fairly settled conditions it ceases
to be injurious, its possessor is under no great
disadvantage, and thus under favourable conditions mathematics is cultivated. Senior
Wranglers may not always be useful members
of society ; but the society that can produce
mathematicians of the quality of the average
Senior Wrangler is likely to have good stuff
in it for success in the struggle with Nature
and with other societies. We must remember
also that, besides the inheritance of a brain,
which by accumulated favourable combinations
of ancestry is capable of high mathematical
thinking, various other conditions are requisite
for the proper development of this capacity.

The art of writing, the Hindoo system of
numerical notation, access to printed text-
books, the opportunity of going to Cambridge,
are all conditions for the development of latent
inherited mathematical capacity.   On the other
hand, suppose a man born even at the present
day with the brains of a Newton (and perhaps
with the feeble body of a Newton also), in the
backwoods of Western America, he would
probably prove a failure, unless he could turn
his gifts to the purposes of commercial speculation : he would be very unlikely to become
an eminent mathematician.

The same arguments will apply in the case
of music.   It is most certainly untrue that
music has not been useful to tribes in their
struggle for existence.   The bard has been no
inconsiderable factor in stimulating the courage
and furthering the cohesion of human societies.
" Let who will make the laws of a nation, let
me make its ballads," said Fletcher of Saltoun ;
and if for " ballads " we put the more general
term " songs," the truth is still more obvious.
The *Marseillaise* and *Die Wacht am Rhein*
count for a good deal in the successes of
French and German armies.   It was not in

vain that, according to the legend (which ex-
presses at least a general truth), the Lace-
dæmonians received from Athens the lame
schoolmaster, who inspired their drooping
courage by his songs ; nor that the militant
Dorians in general understood the value of
music. Music having established its social
utility in this way, there can be no doubt that
sexual selection (in Darwin's sense) would
come in to help the preservation and increase
of any musical talent that appeared. The bard
would be among the first kind of man admired
for some other quality than fighting power or
skill in hunting, and therefore preferred as a
mate. Would not Mr. Wallace's arguments
against the utility of music apply equally to
the songs of birds, and would he not be equally
justified in inferring that the lark and the
nightingale manifest, as certain of our poets
have said, an influx from the spiritual world ?

But, of course, a highly complex music, if it
could have arisen among savages, would be of
no use to them. In order that the great
musician may appear, not only must there be
the physical inheritance of a fortunate combination of musical qualities, but there must be

sufficient leisure and civilisation to save this comparatively rare " variation " from being speedily extinguished ; and he must appear among a people who inherit socially a suffi- cient musical notation and sufficiently complex musical instruments.   Mr. Wallace's objections seem plausible in great measure because he isolates the different forms of intellectual and æsthetic capacity, as if these could exist sepa- rately.   The music of savages is the germ of the music of Beethoven ; but the gap between them is filled by advance, not in music only, but in a vast number of other things.

As to what is quaintly called " the meta- physical faculty," it will be generally agreed that if a man in the Stone Age, instead of sending his flint arrows at something he could eat, had sat down to think how motion was possible, or how contradictory movements were united in his handling of the bow, he would, like his mathematical brother, have supplied the cave-bear with a dinner, and not *vice versâ*. But what appears as metaphysics among races who have won leisure to reflect, and have developed a complex language capable of ex- pressing abstract ideas, had appeared long

before as the mythopœic tendency. This, perhaps, should be called, in Weismann's phrase,
a "bye-product" of the human mind. Reflection about the adaptation of means to ends for
the purpose of everyday life is undoubtedly
useful to the savage; but reflection on these
subjects makes reflection possible on other
subjects also, subjects quite unprofitable at first,
such as "What makes the thunder?" "Why is
the sea salt?" "Why do the flowers come up in
the spring-time?" and so on. And language,
being useful for the communication of practical
projects, serves also to hand down even "useless" myths and legends. Yet are they useless?
They serve to cement the bond between man
and man, and thus have not been crushed out in
the struggle for existence till they come to be a
direct hindrance to progress; and then they disappear before the growth of scientific ideas, except where they linger on as old wives' fables or
children's fairy tales. Yet the crudest mythology
is primitive science and primitive philosophy.

"The peculiar faculty of wit and humour,"
which "appears sporadically in a very small
percentage of the population,"[1] is, we may

[1] *Darwinism*, p. 472.

allow, not useful, except, indeed, in so far as
saying clever things keeps people from doing
foolish ones ; and since wit is only a bye-product of a complex brain, and not a variation
useful to the species, we can easily account for
its sporadic appearance and for the fact that
most men " joke wi' deeficulty." Wit can only
exist where there is a general high average of
brain power, which *is* useful. When life can
be taken with some amount of ease, then, and
only then, do this and the other bye-products
get a chance and escape destruction.

§ 4. *CONCLUSION.*

Thus natural selection, which is a true cause,
seems a perfectly adequate cause to account for
the appearance of all those intellectual capacities of human nature ; and, if social evolution
be rightly understood, there is nothing contradictory to natural selection in the occasional
appearance of very high forms of them. The
spiritual world need not be summoned as a
mysterious counterpart to the material world,
intruding itself into the latter, wherever the
scientific investigator finds a difficulty at first
sight, or the person who is afraid of science

finds a convenient place of refuge for threatened
beliefs. If a spiritual principle is recognised in
the universe, it must be recognised not in the
exceptional, not in holes and corners, like those
intramundane spaces in which Epicurus stowed
away the gods ; but a spiritual principle must
be recognised everywhere, as the condition of
our knowing a system of nature. And Mr.
Wallace is perhaps on the way to a sounder
philosophy when he speaks of even gravitation
as "spiritual," and sees, though dimly, that
mere matter can have no existence, than when
he uses intuitionist arguments about the moral
sense, and treats mathematics and music as
miracles due to a spiritual influx pouring in
like a glacier on the world which is known to
the ordinary biologist. Not in an exceptional
origin of certain rare human qualities, but in
the *nature* of human thought, however origi-
nated, is to be found the true spiritual greatness
of man ; and in the achievements of the human
spirit in the institutions of society, in art, in
religion, in science, and in philosophy is to be
read, if anywhere, the little we can read about
the ultimate meaning of the universe.

III.

NATURAL SELECTION AND THE HISTORY OF INSTITUTIONS.

THE words "Development" and "Evolution" fit the changing course of human
institutions and ideas so well that it seems, and
indeed is, nothing new to find them applied to
history. But there has been a temptation to
assume that the conceptions of biology can be
transferred to the facts of society without the
need of a critical investigation of their validity
in this new sphere. And those who are engaged in historical research regarding special
periods or particular institutions are apt to
resent the procedure of the proudly scientific
sociologist, who simply labels large groups of
facts, taken from different ages and countries,
with some biological heading without having
gone through the labour of investigating concrete details himself. It is so very easy to say
"Evolution" instead of saying "History," and
to use a few Darwinian phrases as keys to

unlock all mysteries. We can understand the
suspicions roused in the mind of the historical
student. But he is a bold man who, in the
name of science, calls himself an "Anti-evolutionist" in these days when even theologians
are endeavouring to make peace with the
conqueror : yet he is performing a useful
function, keeping us from falling into a "dogmatic slumber," and forcing us to analyse the
conceptions we employ.

I propose to examine very briefly some arguments against the applicability of evolutional
theories to the study of social institutions, which
have recently been put forward by an eloquent
Hungarian scholar, Dr. Emil Reich, in a little
book entitled "*Græco-Roman Institutions*,"[1] the
precursor, I believe, of a larger work on the
History of Civilisation. I am not here concerned with Dr. Reich's theories about the
origin of Roman Law, a matter which must be
left to specialists ; nor shall I say anything here
about his underlying philosophical principles.
which seem to me to imply a disbelief both

[1] *Græco-Roman Institutions from an Anti-evolutionist
point of view. Four lectures delivered before the University
of Oxford*, by Emil Reich, Doct. Jur. : Oxford, 1890.

in civilisation and in history.[1] I have to do only with those pages in which he attacks the evolution theory. Furthermore, I am not going to deal with "differentiation" and "integration," the "homogeneous" and the "heterogeneous," or any of the rest of Mr. Herbert Spencer's antithetical formulæ. I shall consider only "the concepts of Darwinism," to which, fortunately for my purpose, Dr. Reich limits his remarks.

Let me then take the factors required by the theory of natural selection, and see in what sense, if in any, they are applicable to society. These are *variation, heredity, struggle for existence.*

§ 2. *"VARIATION."*

In the biological sphere the laws of variation are still to a great extent wrapped in " profound mystery " and the subject of ingenious speculations. When, therefore, some

---

[1] Dr. Reich quotes with approval the dictum of Schopenhauer: " He who has read Herodotus has read all history, the rest being variations on an old theme"—a curious preliminary to a *History of Civilisation.* What would the reader of Herodotus learn about Roman law?

institution, or practice, or idea is called a
"variation" by an evolutionist, the historian
seems to have good ground for his complaint
that nothing is thereby explained, that we
are merely giving a name to the fact and
leaving it as much a mystery as before.[1]   Yet,
if we fully recognise that to say something is
a "spontaneous variation" is only to declare
our ignorance of how it came about, no harm is
done : and it is well to be modest and confess
our ignorance sometimes, though of course
there is no special merit in the mere use of the
Darwinian phrase.   "Instead of begging in-
cipient 'variations,' and leaving the explanation
of their rise entirely unattempted, the *student of
institutions has to insist on nothing more un-
compromisingly, than on the explanation of what
Darwinists call 'variations'*" (p. 68).   An
explanation, certainly, if possible ; but when we
cannot get one, we must go without.   And
what does Dr. Reich understand by an explanation ?   I quote a passage from the next
page :—

---

[1] For the theory of natural selection it is, of course, not
necessary that the causes of a variation should be known.
If the variation is a fact, that is all that is needed.

" Roman law offers, as we saw, the ' variation' of a civil
law saturated with elements of criminal law. The causes
of this variation are perfectly clear to the careful student of
Roman institutions. It was the necessary check of a constitution that was built and erected on the strict morality of
a few citizens " (p. 69).

Dr. Reich does not explain how the variation
arose : he only explains how the variation
proved advantageous to the society in which it
appeared, and so came, in Darwin's phrase, to
be "selected," because it made Rome more
successful than other communities in the
struggle for existence. Dr. Reich claims
(p. 67) to have proved that the Romans "did
not 'evolve' their law out of rudimentary[1]
'variations' aided by 'natural selection in the
struggle for life.'" But, according to what he
says on p. 69, the very thing he has proved
is that Roman law was evolved by natural
selection. He has not used the phrase; but,
what is more important, he has applied the
principle. If we may adopt the convenient
Aristotelian term, Dr. Reich gives the "final
cause," the "what for?" the "good" of an insti-

[1] I suppose Dr. Reich means "variations which are
rudiments."

tution : he does not give its "efficient cause," he does not explain how the first germs of the institution came into being, any more than an evolutionist who uses the phrase "spontaneous variation."

In the case of the higher plants and animals, an undoubted cause of variation is *sex*. It is almost universally conceded that where two parents are needed, instead of one, there is a new combination of elements and a consequent possibility of variation at every step in descent. To produce the same apple we have to avoid sexual reproduction ; seedlings mean the likelihood of new varieties. Direct action of the environment is an undoubted cause of variation in protozoa ; whether it also affects *species* produced by sexual reproduction is the controversy of the day among biologists.[1] (Of course it affects all *individuals*.)

Now does anything correspond to "sex" and to "the direct action of the environment" in the case of societies, institutions, customs ? The environment most certainly does act upon races in determining their mode of life. Geographical conditions—mountains, plains or sea

[1] See above, pp. 42, 88.

—climate, the fauna and flora of the district, are all causes of variations. The change produced in the English race by America and Australia is a good instance.[1] Whether and in what way the effects of climate, etc., on the physical organism are directly transmitted by heredity is, of course, part of controversy just referred to. Natural selection produces such an adaptation of the physical organism as is necessary to survival, *i.e.*, types of physique that are not adapted to the new conditions die out, and so the more suitable types are constantly selected, and thus there may gradually arise a great deviation from the type which remains more or less persistent in the old surroundings. Whether, over and above this gradual change produced by natural selection, the very marked effects which take place in the individual's lifetime are transmitted to his posterity is, as we have said, as yet " not proven."

But does anything correspond to " sex" ? Here, of course would be a tempting opportunity for the political psychologist, like Bluntschli,[2]

[1] Cp. Sir Chas. Dilke, *Problems of Greater Britain*, ii. p. 579.

[2] *Theory of the State*, Engl. Transl., p. 22.

who tells us that the State is male, and the Church female (an opinion greatly supported, if not suggested, by the genders of the German words), or by those who speak of the Teutons as a masculine race, and the Celts as a feminine, and so on. But we need not spend time on these grammatical or poetical fancies. It is very generally admitted that sex, as a cause for variation, means mixture of elements ; and thus its equivalent in social evolution is mingling of races and all that that brings with it. The Hellenic colonies in Asia and Africa supply abundant examples of the great variations brought about in character, institutions and ideas through the mixture of stocks. Our own race is another conspicuous example ; and our language is a " variation " issuing from the marriage of a Low German speech with one of the children of Latin.

Apart altogether from the production of a " mixed race," there may be an intermingling of ideas and customs. Here we come upon the differences between organic and superorganic evolution. Human beings are not dependent on heredity alone. They may unconsciously or consciously imitate one another. At the

lowest stage there is the childish copying of
strange modes of dress and habits, which is so
common among savages and in fashionable
society—doing a thing simply because others
do it without any *reason* for it. Higher than
this comes that learning from enemies which
made the Romans struggling with the Cartha-
ginians become a naval power through conscious imitation for a deliberate purpose.
When they came in contact with the Greeks,
their old customs began to vary, and they
learnt much good and some evil. It is more
than a mere figure of speech if we call Virgil's
poetry the offspring of a marriage between
Italy and Greece. Similarly the Alexandrian
culture was the child of East and West. Even
temporary contact, whether of alliance or
hostility, may produce lasting effects. The
Crusaders brought back Saracenic culture to the
western world. The Peninsular war introduced
cigars into England ; the Crimean war introduced cigarettes. These were new "variations"
in England. The effect of contact is generally
some compromise—some product that is altogether new, the child, not of one parent, but of
two, or of many.

On the other hand, the legislators of ancient Lacedæmon knew (like the Chinese) that, to keep institutions from varying, they must exclude foreign influences. Greek political idealists, who dreaded change above everything, feared the very neighbourhood of the sea.[1] Here we have the equivalent of the identity of type which is maintained in plants where sexual reproduction is avoided.

The success of mixed races (provided the mixture be a good one), the advantage which has often come to a country even from conflict, are to a great extent to be explained by the additional chances of favourable variations which such races possess over those who are living on with the same stock of blood, institutions and ideas. " Protestant variations " at least imply intellectual progress. The absence of dissent and of controversy (which is the conflict and mingling of different ideas) means intellectual sterility. The Jews have remained the same race more than any other people ; but they form no exception, for they have been dwellers in many lands, and whilst strengthened by the persecutions, they have been enriched by

[1] Cp. Plato, *Laws*, 704, 705.

the ideas, as well as by the trade, of many nations.
Even the Roman Church, whilst boasting its
unity and its permanence, has learnt much and
gained much from conflict with its Protestant
rivals.

When we explain a "variation" by referring
it simply to race, we are not explaining it at all;
and it is well to have this pointed out. To
explain Roman institutions by the national
character of the Romans is, as Dr. Reich says
(p. 17), just like explaining phenomena by
means of "occult qualities." People in general
are far too ready to refer the differences they
find between nations to race-characteristics, instead of taking the trouble to look for other
explanations first, in geographical conditions,
institutions, past history and other external influences. Only when we have eliminated what
is due to any or all of these causes (if we ever
can do this), are we entitled to ascribe the resi-
dual phenomena solely to race-characteristics.
English people have been very apt to explain
all Irish discontents by saying that they result
from the Irish, or, to make it look more scientific, from the "Celtic" character; this is more
convenient than to read some very unpleasant

D.P.   K

pages of history and to trace the consequences
of political oppression. An ethnological explanation is *as yet* no explanation, but only a
re-statement of the problem to be solved.

Social variations may arise, then, from external influences, from intermixture or contact
of races, from more or less conscious imitation. Conscious imitation because of some
expected advantage already implies reflection,
which is a further cause of variation among
human beings. If customs or institutions are
adopted not unconsciously, but because a re-
forming party have felt, and have convinced
others, that such a change would be more
advantageous to the community than to abide
by the old customs, this is a variation resulting
from reflection. Like all other variations, it
will not become fixed as the characteristic of
a type, unless it prove advantageous in some
way or other, and for some time; it differs
from other variations in being adopted expressly because of its anticipated utility.

We are indeed very apt to imagine that many
variations, which have proved advantageous
because of some purpose they serve, arose at
first because of this advantage. We are often

obliged for convenience to speak as if this were so ; as, for instance, when we speak of " mimicry " in insects. This anticipatory mode of expression may cause no harm when applied to the lower animals, though even there it is apt to mislead the uninformed. In the case of human society it is always treacherous : it suggests the opposite exaggeration to that of those who see in human society nothing but mere natural processes and deny the place of deliberate reflection altogether. The distribution of powers which Montesquieu saw and admired in the English constitution was not the result of reflection on the part of any legislator ; the distribution of powers which the founders of the American constitution adopted from Montesquieu's version of the English constitution was due to reflection.

§ 3. "*HEREDITY.*"

By heredity in biological evolution is meant the fact that spontaneous variations tend to persist in the race, to be transmitted by descent. But human beings, besides sharing in this biological transmission of inherited characteristics, have also other modes of transmitting sentiments and customs ; they are not dependent merely on heredity in the biological sense. They can "inherit" by means of language and institutions the experience of their ancestors, which would otherwise be lost and have to be acquired afresh—unless of course the Lamarckian hypothesis were true. A conspicuous example of the extent to which "social" inheritance may go, entirely unaided by biological inheritance, is to be found in the persistence of type and character in the Catholic clergy. There may even be less change in a celibate than in a hereditary official class. " Le clergé," says Montesquieu, " est une famille qui ne peut pas périr."

This capacity of social inheritance is *the* great advantage that mankind possesses over the brutes ; and the greater perfection in the modes of transmitting experience constitutes the advantage of civilised over uncivilised races. I have already suggested a definition of civilisation as " the sum of those contrivances which enable human beings to advance independently of [biological] heredity." [1]

[1] See above, p. 101.

In biological heredity structures are preserved and improved, if they are of distinct
advantage to the species, through the operation
of natural selection. If they cease to be of
use, they may still persist as "survivals," unless
they come to be of such decided disadvantage
to the species that they disappear through
natural selection. The same holds, *mutatis
mutandis*, in sociological inheritance, and "survivals" may be found in abundance. Some of
these may be retained because they serve a
purpose very different from that served by the
original variation from which they are de-
scended.

Dr. Reich objects very strongly to the theory
of "survivals" as applied to institutions and
customs. " Our view of institutions " he says
(p. 70) " being that all *present* institutions are
kept in existence by *present* causes, we cannot
adopt the evolutionist views of ' survivals.'
Odd habits and ceremonies of our age, for
instance, that are commonly explained on the
assumption of their being ' survivals ' of former
ages, can all be accounted for by the working
of present, *if latent*, causes." Here, as before,
Dr. Reich recognises a " final cause," but

refuses to recognise an "efficient" or "material"
cause. Now, surely, a *complete* account of any
institution would tell us not only what purpose
that institution now serves, but what it came
from ; we need a theory of origin as well as an
explanation of present value. But Dr. Reich's
view of causation is peculiar in this respect.
Thus he says (on p. 19) : "The Americans
continue to observe their written constitution,
not because it was once written, but because
they are determined to revere it as their funda-
mental law. It is their merit, not that of
Jefferson or Washington." Surely, if we are
fully to understand the American constitution,
we must take account of the makers of the
constitution, its sources and the circumstances
in which it came into existence, as well as of
the present feelings of the law-abiding citizens
of the United States. There is, indeed, an
unfortunate quarrel between the "historical"
and the "analytic" methods of dealing with
institutions. Voltaire ridiculed Montesquieu
for saying that the English constitution came
from the forests of barbarous Germany. "I
might as well say that the sermons of Tillotson
and Smalridge were composed of old by

Teutonic witches who divined the success of a war by the way in which the blood ran from the veins of a sacrificed captive." To say this may not seem quite so absurd to us as it did to Voltaire. A scientific student of religions might trace a connection between primitive magic and human sacrifice on the one hand and even tolerably advanced forms of Christian theology on the other. Professor Dicey does not think it necessary, like Mr. Freeman, to bring in the *Landesgemeinden* of Uri, the witness of Homer, the *Germania* of Tacitus, or the constitution of the Witenagemót, in explaining the British constitution as that now is.[1] The constitutional lawyer has a different problem from that of the historical antiquarian : and it is well to have it pointed out that we must explain an institution by considering not only what it came out of, but the way in which it now exists and the purposes it now serves. As we have said, a complete explanation requires both an investigation of origins (material and efficient causes) and an investigation of present nature and functions (formal and final causes). Let me take one other illustration of what I

---

[1] Dicey, *Law of the Constitution*, pp. viii. 13 ff. (Ed. 3).

mean, as it is a very excellent one. How are
we to explain the absence of the English
sovereign from Cabinet Councils ? Of course
it might be answered, and I imagine Dr. Reich
would answer, that the present character of the
English constitution requires that the sovereign should have no personal responsibility
for the policy adopted by the ministry. But
the explanation is surely incomplete, if we do
not take account of the fact that George I.
could not speak English, and consequently left
his ministers to deliberate by themselves.
Here was an "accidental" variation, which,
proving favourable, gave rise to what now forms
an essential principle of the constitution.

To come specially to "survivals." If we were
to allege *e.g.* the use of Norman-French in
giving the royal assent to acts of Parliament
as an example of a survival, Dr. Reich, I suppose, would answer that this is kept up for the
sake of maintaining the dignity of the Crown.
Use plain English and the monarchy would
tumble to pieces. Let us allow this to be the
case : we know that it is generally risky to
meddle with a very ancient piece of furniture.
But surely a scientific explanation of this

custom would require some reference to the
Norman Conquest. Again, if we were to point
to the shape of the academic dress worn in
Oxford and Cambridge, Dr. Reich would
answer that this is kept up for the sake of
proctorial discipline. Granted that *a* uniform
is kept up for the purpose; but why this particular uniform? A glance at an academic
fashion-plate of the seventeenth century will
supply an answer, so far as the square cap is
concerned. There we see this cap in a shape
exactly intermediate between the clerical
berretta and its present form.

In scientific explanation it is not enough to
show why some sort of thing exists or is done :
we must explain, if we can, why it is just *this*
and no other. The biologist does not merely
say that colours of animals are useful to them,
in the way of protection, etc.; if he says this, he
is bound to show why this particular arrange-
ment of stripes or spots is useful to this particular species in its particular environment ;
and if he calls anything a " survival," he must
not be satisfied till he can show from what
previous condition it is a survival. And so, it
is not from a desire to take refuge in a vague

general term, but because we are looking for concrete particular explanations, that we insist on the reality of "survivals" in institutions. The fact that a custom occasionally outlives the conditions which originally favoured its growth, needs no explanation. The tendency of human beings is to go on doing what they have been accustomed to do, unless there is a very strong reason for giving it up; and frequently even then. Natural selection does not eliminate disadvantageous customs in coherent human societies as rapidly as it eliminates disadvantageous characteristics among the lower animals. The disappearance of the circumstances, which produced any particular custom originally, make it easy, of course, fc r the custom to die out; but, as a rule, some positive and considerable inconvenience is necessary to rouse people sufficiently to make them shake off any old habit. Occasionally something purely "accidental" ("accidental," of course, only in the same sense in which we speak of "spontaneous" variations) is sufficient to put an end to an old custom : thus the death of the holder of some antiquated office may give the occasion for discontinuing it. If an old custom dies out gradually, because it has ceased to have a meaning and a value, that is an illustration of the cessation of natural selection : if it becomes positively hurtful, it may lead to the destruction of the society that observes it, unless a wise change anticipates the operation of natural selection.

§ 4. *" THE STRUGGLE FOR EXISTENCE."*

Most of what would fall to be said on this subject has already been discussed in the two preceding essays :[1] and therefore a very brief summary of results must suffice here. First of all, the units engaged in that struggle which constitutes human history are not individuals only, but aggregates of individuals, such as tribes, races, nations, classes, sects. Secondly, apart from the struggle between individual and individual, between race and race, nation and nation, there is a struggle between institutions, languages, ideas. From these differences, in degree of complexity, between the biological and the sociological meaning of " struggle for existence " there follow two consequences : (1) The death of the individual organism is not

[1] Cp. pp. 13 ff., 97 ff.

always necessary in "sociological" natural
selection. "Evolutionist theories," says Dr.
Reich, "draw most heavily on 'death"; and
so they must, because nature is "careless of
the single life." And in the case of social
organisms death is at work too; but the individuals of unsuccessful social organisms do not
necessarily perish. The extinction of the individual is not always required for the triumph
of an idea.[1]   (2) On the other hand, ideas
and institutions may outlive individuals and
societies. Roman law has outlived all the
Roman lawyers and the Roman Empire itself.
Thus it is no argument whatever against the
applicability of the doctrine of natural selection
to social institutions to suggest, as Dr. Reich
does, that an evolutionist historian must always
hold that every later stage must be superior to
the preceding, simply because it has "survived."

[1] Cp. S. Alexander, *Moral Order and Progress*, p. 330.
"Punishment in man corresponds to the struggle of the
dominant variety with other varieties. . .' . We punish
in order to extirpate ideals which offend the dominant or
general ideal. But in nature conflict means the extinction
of individual animals: in punishment, it is sufficient that
the false ideal is extinguished, and it is not necessary always
that the person himself should be destroyed."

"Survival of the fittest" is a very ambiguous phrase ; and degeneration is often a condition of survival, instead of progress.

I have thus tried to show that the "concepts of Darwinism" are perfectly applicable to human society *mutatis mutandis.* The quali-fication is essential. The uncritical use of biological formulæ only leads to bad results in sociology and in practical politics. The genuinely scientific historian may never men-tion a single evolutionist catch-word, and yet be contributing to our knowledge of Evolution in its highest phase. The philosopher who saw a dialectic movement in human history and in the whole process of the universe was only reading back into the lower stages of Evolution what comes clearly to the surface in the highest, where the blind conflict of nature passes over into the conscious conflict of ideas. Progress comes only by struggle, though the struggle in its highest form may go on within the in-dividual soul and may cause no death but the death of partial truths that have become errors, and of customs that have outlived their use.

Butler & Tanner, The Selwood Printing Works, Frome, and London.

SOME PRESS NOTICES ON THE FIRST EDITION
OF "DARWINISM AND POLITICS."

" This very able and interesting essay."—*Glasgow Herald.*

" Will be found suggestive throughout."—*Pall Mall Gazette.*

" Considerable ingenuity as well as originality."—*Whitehall Review.*

" Represents very well the attitude of many of the most earnest and cultured men at present guiding the destinies of the ancient Universities."—*Manchester Examiner.*

" Among the thoughtful books of 1889, we can recommend this little volume."—*True Thinker.*

"A bright healthy piece of philosophy, with touches of pleasant humour."—*Inquirer.*

" Extremely suggestive and full of valuable ideas for the philosophic student of sociology."—*Woman's World.*

" One of the most suggestive books that we have met with for some time past, and we cannot commend it too highly to our readers."—*Literary World.*

"A timely criticism of the application of biological conceptions to social problems."—*Political Science Quarterly.*

" Short, crisp, argumentative, and practical."—*Critic.*

" Numerous as books on political and social economy now are, Mr. Ritchie's volume should certainly not be overlooked."—*British Weekly.*

SOCIAL SCIENCE SERIES.

Scarlet Cloth, each 2s. 6d.

1. **WORK AND WAGES.** Prof. J. E. THOROLD ROGERS.
   " Nothing that Professor Rogers writes can fail to be of interest to thoughtful people."—*Athenæum.*

2. **CIVILISATION: Its Cause and Cure.** EDWARD CARPENTER.
   " No passing piece of polemics, but a permanent possession."—*Scottish Review.*

3. **QUINTESSENCE OF SOCIALISM.** Dr. SCHÄFFLE.
   " Precisely the manual needed. Brief, lucid, fair, and wise."—*British Weekly.*

4. **DARWINISM AND POLITICS.** D. G. RITCHIE, M.A.
   (Oxon.) With an Appendix, showing its applications to (1) The Labour Question ; (2) The Position of Women ; (3) The Population Question. Second Edition, with two New Essays on Human Evolution.
   " One of the most suggestive books we have met with."—*Literary World.*

5. **RELIGION OF SOCIALISM.** E. BELFORT BAX.

6. **ETHICS OF SOCIALISM.** E. BELFORT BAX.
   " Mr. Bax is by far the ablest of the English exponents of Socialism.' —*Westminster Review*

7. **THE DRINK QUESTION.** Dr. KATE MITCHELL.
   " Plenty of interesting matter for reflection." - *Graphic.*

8. **PROMOTION OF GENERAL HAPPINESS.** Prof. M. MACMILLAN.
   " A reasoned account of the most advanced and most enlightened utilitarian doctrine in a clear and readable form."—*Scotsman.*

9. **ENGLAND'S IDEAL, Etc.** EDWARD CARPENTER.
   " The literary power is unmistakable, their freshness of style, their humour, and their enthusiasm."—*Pall Mall.*

10. **SOCIALISM IN ENGLAND.** SIDNEY WEBB, LL.B.
    " The best general view of the subject from the moderate Socialist side."—*Athenæum.*

11. **PRINCE BISMARCK AND STATE SOCIALISM.** W. H. DAWSON.
    " A succinct, well-digested review of German social and economic legislation since 1870."—*Saturday Review.*

12. **GODWIN'S POLITICAL JUSTICE (ON PROPERTY).** Edited by H. S. SALT.
    " Shows Godwin at his best ; with an interesting and informing Introduction."—*Glasgow Herald.*

13. **STORY OF THE FRENCH REVOLUTION.** E. BELFORT BAX.
    " A trustworthy outline."—*Scotsman.*

14. **THE CO-OPERATIVE COMMONWEALTH.** LAURENCE GRONLUND.
    " An independent exposition of the Socialism of the Marx School."—*Contemporary Review.*

SOCIAL SCIENCE SERIES—*continued.*

15. **ESSAYS AND ADDRESSES.** BERNARD BOSANQUET, M.A. (Oxon.)

"Ought to be in the hands of every student of the Nineteenth Century spirit."—*Echo.*
"No one can complain of not being able to understand what Mr. Bosanquet means."—*Pall Mall Gazette.*

16. **CHARITY ORGANISATION.** C. S. LOCH, Secretary to Charity Organisation Society.

"A perfect little manual."—*Athenæum.*
"Deserves a wide circulation."—*Scotsman.*

17. **THOREAU'S ANTI-SLAVERY AND REFORM PAPERS.** Edited by H. S. SALT.

18. **SELF-HELP A HUNDRED YEARS AGO.** G. J. HOLYOAKE.

19. **THE NEW YORK STATE REFORMATORY AT ELMIRA.** ALEXANDER WINTER; with Preface by HAVELOCK ELLIS.

20. **COMMON-SENSE ABOUT WOMEN.** T. W. HIGGINSON.

21. **THE UNEARNED INCREMENT.** W. H. DAWSON.

22. **OUR DESTINY.** LAURENCE GRONLUND.

23. **THE WORKING-CLASS MOVEMENT IN AMERICA.** Dr. ED. and E. MARX AVELING.

24. **LUXURY.** EMILE DE LAVELEYE.

25. **THE LAND AND THE LABOURERS.** Rev. C. W. STUBBS, M.A.

IN ACTIVE PREPARATION ARE:—

ORIGIN OF PROPERTY IN LAND. FUSTEL DE COULANGES. Edited by Prof. ASHLEY.

MALTHUS'S ESSAY ON POPULATION. Edited by A. K. DONALD.

THE CO-OPERATIVE MOVEMENT. BEATRICE POTTER.

THE STUDENT'S MARX: An Abridgement of his "Capital."

LANGE'S THE LABOUR PROBLEM. Translated by Rev. J. CARTER.

CRIME AND THE PRISON SYSTEM. W. DOUGLAS MORRISON.

PRINCIPLES OF STATE INTERFERENCE. D. G. RITCHIE, M.A.

THE EVOLUTION OF PROPERTY. PAUL LAFARGUE.

LONDON: SWAN SONNENSCHEIN & CO.